Jews Clues:
You're Doing It All Wrong

Unsolicited Advice,
Unwanted Opinions and
Unlikely Anecdotes

By:

C. J. Kaplan
&
Mitch Blum

Special thanks to:

Cover Design: Scott Combs
(sscombs@me.com)

Photographer: Steven Piet
(stevenpiet@gmail.com)

Production Company: Sarofsky Corp.
(www.sarofsky.com)

TABLE OF CONTENTS

With much love to both of our families

Whatever didn't kill us just made us crazier

FORWARD

Only .2% of the world is born Jewish. That means a whopping 99.8% of the population is wandering around without any idea how to live their lives.

The tiny Semitic minority, on the other hand, has been told exactly what to do and how to do it since the day they were born. The source of this burning bush-like guidance is always - almost without exception - the Jewish mother.

Now, the Jewish mother has very clear cut career and social goals for her child from the time that child enters pre-school. She has also meticulously outlined the path by which said child will achieve those goals. All the stupid kid has to do is follow her endless stream of advice, edicts, feedback and directives and success is guaranteed.

Despite the Jewish mother's best efforts, though, many children learn to think for themselves. They go off and become rock stars and artists instead of doctors and lawyers and end up marrying for love instead of compatibility on J-Date. Hence the Jewish mother's eternal lament that her children NEVER LISTEN TO A WORD SHE SAYS.

Well, this is a book written by two children who did listen. And not only did they listen but, unfortunately for their mothers, they also wrote everything down.

Jews Clues is a unapologetic compendium of motherly advice strained through the wry and sardonic filter of the sons who received it. Each entry provides insight into the seemingly arbitrary, frequently ridiculous, sometimes contradictory instructions that have been handed down from generation to generation, one pointed criticism at a time.

Filled with nearly 300 Clues (smart-ass aphorisms touching on multiple subjects), over 100 Chai-Kus (Jewish-themed Haikus) and 16 humorous essays, this book captures the American Jewish angst like no other.

Whether you're Jewish or not, *Jews Clues* is the easiest, funniest way to experience what it's like to grow up with a Jewish mother. And though it's probably too late for the authors, a cover to cover reading of this tome may stop you from being a source of shame to your family.

So, go ahead, dive in. To paraphrase our mothers, you'll thank us later.

*

PART 1: JEWS CLUES

Do what we say, not what we do

Food & Drink

Nova, not belly.

*

Restaurant Rule: appetizers or dessert.
Never both. Preferably neither.

*

Israel has been invaded hundreds of times
throughout history.
And yet, the only thing we've ever invaded
is a buffet.

*

"Just a sliver" is Jewish code for
"I'd like another large piece of cake without
any commentary, thank you."

*

Kosher deli: triumphant.
Kosher pizza: tragic.

*

Yes, you can put peanut butter on a bagel.
But, why would you?

*

Only your mother and the Girl Scouts can guilt you
into eating something you shouldn't.

*

In many Kosher homes, there is a loophole known as
"the paper plate."

*

"Neufchatel" is French for
"really crappy cream cheese."

*

Dear Starbucks,
Love the coffee. But, please, let's end this
charade with the bagels.

*

Any time someone tells me they think
certain Jewish foods are gross,
I have two words for them: egg and nog.

*

Never eat deviled eggs unless you can verify that they
were made within the last 30 seconds.

*

The Yiddish word "pupik" was created
so we could eat sketchy parts of the turkey
without sounding disgusting.

*

Ironically, our "forbidden fruit" is cheese steak.

*

You call this a Bed & Breakfast?
Where's the omelet station?

*

If chicken soup is Jewish penicillin,
then Slivovitz is Jewish painkiller.

*

Butter can be used as a topping, as a baking
ingredient and as a way to describe an exceptionally
comfortable leather sofa.

*

The greatest achievement in any Jew's life is finally
getting "the hug" from the maitre d' at the local
Chinese restaurant.

*

You have bologna. We have salami.
Can't we all just get along?

*

Pork. The forbidden white meat.

*

Many Jews are retiring to Arizona instead of Florida.
What do they do for bagels?

*

You can't put mayonnaise on pastrami.
You just can't.

*

Bagels are one of the greatest gifts given by Jews to
the rest of mankind.
But we're keeping bialys all to ourselves.

*

The difference between a Kosher deli
and a Kosher-style deli:
Cheese blintzes vs. Cheeseburgers.

*

The pious man grills Hebrew Nationals.
The wise man grills Pearls.

*

The Jewish "Happy Meal":
A sandwich packed from home
and a toy from the dollar store.

*

The guilt-ridden phrase, "What am I, chopped liver?"
is largely ineffective because
most Jews love chopped liver.

*

Keep a couple of Ziploc bags in your purse
in case you want to bring a few items
home from the buffet for later.

*

Sushi is gross.
But, stuffed intestine…now that's good eating.

*

In a Jewish kitchen there's a fine line
between moldy bread and "toast."

*

Superman has kryptonite.
Eastern European Jews have milk.

*

Jews are single-handedly responsible for destroying
the MSG industry.

*

The Jews and the Italians are the only people
who can be trusted to run a deli properly.

*

It was a dark day for Jewish cuisine when doctors
came out against salt.

*

Every meal at a Chinese restaurant must commence
with a complaint about how they don't provide free
fried noodles anymore.

*

Even if it's cooked perfectly, send it back.

*

Nobody knows if Dr. Brown is a real doctor,
but he sure makes the finest Black Cherry and
Cel-Ray soda in the world.

*

Cream cheese and ketchup can be combined to make
a sauce that's as good as or better than any marinara.

*

Chinese food is best enjoyed on Sundays.
Or whatever day Christmas Eve happens to fall.

*

Affairs (the good kind)

Jewish affair timeline:
1) Pre-affair dinner
2) Affair
3) Post-affair brunch
4) Post-brunch calls to criticize your relatives

*

You've made a memory glass:
70% chance you're Jewish.
You've received a memory glass:
100% chance you're Jewish.

*

At most weddings, the line at the bar is 10 deep.
At Jewish weddings, the line at the buffet is 10 deep.

*

After seeing what my friends paid
for their daughter's Bat-Mitzvah,
I'm realizing that I should have become a caterer.
Or an Episcopalian.

*

Any random relative can light the candles
at a wedding or Bar-Mitzvah,
but your grandfather has to do
the blessing over the challah.

*

At the next cocktail hour, position yourself near the
kitchen doors so you can get to the appetizers before
the other schnorrers.

*

One day an enterprising Jew will invent a chair
seatbelt to prevent Hora-related injuries.

*

A free meal at Denny's,
a free coffee at Starbucks,
a free cone at Baskin-Robbins.
Now that's what makes birthdays special.

*

The highest compliment you can pay
the bride's parents:
"Who's your caterer?"

*

The fancier the affair, the larger the shrimp served
during the cocktail hour.

*

If you get bar mitzvah'd on a Saturday night
you won't have to do a Haftorah portion.
Just sayin'.

*

Regardless of the fact that 99% of writing
is now done with a keyboard,
you will still get five to ten Cross pen sets
for your Bar-Mitzvah.

*

Fashion & Style

Some guys look good with a pierced ear.
None of those guys are Jewish.

*

It is possible to bring shame and dishonor upon your
entire family by wearing an old shirt or faded pair of
jeans out in public.

*

The difference between a nose job and a boob job?
Your parents will pay for your nose job.

*

If you're under 60 and wearing a track suit,
you'd better be training for the Boston Marathon.

*

Three things you will never see in a synagogue:
pork, crosses, Ed Hardy tee shirts.

*

Our moms always railed against animal cruelty.
The minks that comprised their winter coats
must have died of old age.

*

Is it just me or did anyone else think
Abercrombie & Fitch was a goyisha law firm?

*

Hello unsexy winter pajamas.
Goodbye unsexy summer pajamas.

*

There's never been a Jewish grandchild whose hair
wasn't too long or too short.

*

Wal-Mart. How can a place with such great prices be
so incredibly non-Jewish?

*

Such a pretty girl. Why all the piercings?

*

At a certain age Jewish women stop getting
their hair cut at salons and start getting
their hair set at beauty parlors.

*

This humidity is making my sideburns frizzy.

*

I know this guy in the Jewelry District…

*

It's hot!
Watch yourself on those plastic seat covers.

*

It's Jewish law that when women reach menopause
they must dye their hair red.

*

Regardless of body type or volume of chest hair, be
sure to open the top 3 or 4 buttons of your shirt.
Especially in a casino.

*

Long before it became popular to wear track suits,
Jewish grandmothers were rocking the
Sergio Tacchinis down in FLA.

*

Natural blonde. For Jewish women, there is no bigger
contradiction in terms.

*

Gold necklaces for men never go out of style.

*

Sports

A Jewish perfect game:
free tickets, free parking, free bobblehead doll.

*

Jews are like Red Sox fans.
Neither is happy unless there's something to
complain about.

*

The Jewish Marathon:
Driving from Boston to New York
without stopping to pee.

*

Jews watch football on TV, go to football games
and even own football teams.
But under no circumstances do Jews
actually PLAY football.

*

My mom thinks March Madness
is a spring sale at Loehmann's.

*

If Bridge ever takes off like Poker did
we'll finally have a sport we can dominate.

*

With Spring Training starting next week,
Florida Jews finally have something
to yell at besides each other.

*

This year, there are five basketball games and one
football game on Christmas Day.
I guess there really is a Santa Claus.

*

Baseball's free agency period:
when Jews really become involved
in professional sports.

*

In non-Jewish sports news, hockey season has started.

*

Driving Sunday School carpool shows your
commitment to Jewish education.
And gives you time to place a few
football bets as well.

*

There comes a time in every Jewish family,
no matter how devout, when they decide
to watch sports on Yom Kippur.

*

When Yom Kippur falls on a Saturday, many high
school golf and tennis teams are left shorthanded.
High school football teams remain unaffected.

*

There is nothing more honorable than refusing to play
professional sports on the High Holidays.
Unless your team loses.

*

My Dad was going to play in the British Open
this year but he couldn't get his golf cart
shipped over from Florida.

*

Jews don't care much for soccer.
We have no use for a conflict that ends in a tie.

*

In the soccer World Cup,
one man's vuvuzela is another man's shofar.

*

Rules for Children

You can be anything your mother wants you to be.

*

There is always one side of the family
that you don't speak to anymore.
And it's their fault.

*

Jews don't get divorced. That's too easy.
A good Jewish marriage requires years of bickering to
be considered a success.

*

When it comes to paying for movie tickets, there's
never been a Jewish grandchild over 4 years old.

*

If we get any more snow, the neighborhood kids
who shovel my driveway are going to start
demanding 401(k) plans.

*

If I had a nickel for every time my parents
gave my kids a dollar…

*

Sorry kids, you can't cash the checks until
you write the thank-you notes.

*

There's no way I'm paying those neighborhood kids
snow shoveling prices just for raking leaves.

*

You can never have too many pairs of socks.

*

No, you can't drink coffee – it'll stunt your growth.

*

You're only going to get one soda per meal.
So if you drink it all before your food comes,
that's your problem, mister.

*

If someone slighted you in the third grade, never, ever
forgive them as long as you live.

*

Don't get smart with me.

*

You're not allowed to order soda at
Chinese restaurants. If you're thirsty,
enjoy the complimentary tea and water.

*

For Jews, there is always a "proper way" to do things.
Not surprisingly, the proper way is always
your mother's way.

*

You should be more like your brother.

*

At this very moment, you are breaking
your mother's heart and/or killing your father.

*

Just because no one is using the shuffleboard court or
the pool at your grandparent's condo doesn't mean
that you can.

*

It doesn't matter if other people's
children are doing it.
You are not other people's children.

*

Agree with everything your parents say.
It will confuse them long enough for you to do
whatever you want.

*

"In point five miles, turn left.
Or don't if you think you know better, Mr. Big Shot.
See if I care."
(If my mom were the voice of the GPS.)

*

Living at home was like prison in that you'd
occasionally get your room tossed
for cigarettes and porn.

*

"We didn't know any better."
What your parents say when you remind them of the
horrible things they did during your childhood.

*

Anything your mother does to piss you off will be
justified by your father with the phrase:
"She does it out of love."

*

Before: "Get off your tuchus and do
something with your life!"
After: "What? Too busy to call your mother?"

*

"If I had spoken to your grandfather that way, you
and I wouldn't be alive to have this conversation."

*

Rules for Adults

Two things you should do when you get engaged:
1) Call your family
2) Get the ring appraised
(Not necessarily in that order.)

*

Never buy a German car.
(Unless you really, really want it.)

*

A gift to a woman for giving birth
is called a "push present."
A gift to a Jewish woman for giving birth
is called a "diamond."

*

"So, I see you're getting some snow."
(Florida retiree trash talk.)

*

The older your grandparents get, the more dirt they're
willing to spill about your parents.

*

Go ahead and say what's on your mind.
You can always apologize later.

*

Two weeks into winter and I'm already wondering
about the lowest age it would be socially acceptable
to move to Florida.

*

It's time to invite those neighbors with the
snow blower over for coffee.

*

Mistletoe is hit or miss. But if you stand underneath a
diamond necklace, your chances of getting some
action increase exponentially.

*

Love is always having to say you're sorry.

*

If you think helping your kids with their homework makes you feel stupid, wait until they bring you their Hebrew School assignments.

*

You don't have to do what your parents say, but you do have to pretend to listen to their opinion.

*

Sure, you could pay for a visit to the eye doctor, but the off-the-rack reading glasses at the drugstore work just as well.

*

There will always be at least one room in your parent's home that nobody is allowed to enter.

*

Don't own a boat. Have a friend who owns a boat.

*

Keep your friends close and your enemies closer.
And your parents at least an hour away by car.

*

Never display paperback books in your library –
they make you look cheap.

*

If you're not having a good time, it's your obligation
to make sure nobody else is either.

*

In life there are successful people and then there are
people who aren't doctors or lawyers.

*

You need to tidy up before
the cleaning people get here.

*

Keep your home extremely hot or extremely cold.
Never settle for a happy medium.

*

Yelling is not only an acceptable form of
communication, it is preferred.

*

The ironic thing about Jewish living rooms is that no
living being is allowed to sit on the couch.

*

Boynton Beach, West Palm and Boca Raton: Yes.
Tallahassee, St. Petersburg and Pensacola:
Not so much.

*

Thinning hair doesn't bother me.
It's the fact that I can't get the barber to pro-rate my
haircut that's so upsetting.

*

Old Jewish men get out of bed 5 times a night to pee,
but can somehow sleep through two football games
on the couch dry as a bone.

*

In the next few weeks, the birds and the Jews will
begin to migrate south.

*

What's all this sudden fascination with vampires?
My good-for-nothing children have been sucking me
dry for years.

*

Who do you trust more: the restaurant's computer or
an old Jewish man without his reading glasses
adding up the check in his head?

*

Salutatorian? Feh.
My friend's grandson was valedictorian.

*

No, you're not crazy.
That valet really did want to steal
the change out of your ashtray.

*

Holidays

NEW YEAR'S

Didn't we already do this whole New Year's
thing a few months back?

*

TU B'SHEVAT

Told my boss I was taking the day off
for Tu B'Shevat.
It sounded more legit than saying I'd be out
for Jewish Arbor Day.

*

VALENTINE'S DAY

I doubt that Valentine's Day was created by a saint.
More likely some guy named Schwartz in the
marketing department at Hallmark.

*

ST. PATRICK'S DAY

Any holiday centered around corned beef
is okay by us.

*

PASSOVER

The older the leader of your Seder is, the closer to his
chair the afikomen will be.

*

The Jews wandered through the desert for 40 years.
Yet, our parents still refuse to use the GPS.

*

If you like chocolate, Passover is your holiday.
Unless you like good chocolate.
Then you're in for a rough week.

*

Contrary to popular belief, the hardest part about
Passover isn't the food.
It's the Manischewitz hangovers.

*

Haggadah: Charoset recalls the mortar the Israelites
used to bond bricks.
My Dad: That's what it feels like in your colon too.

*

Our second Seder is way more lax.
My father-in-law skips certain prayers by saying,
"Well, you remember that from last night."

*

Which grandparent will be the first to make the
"Boy, is Elijah going to be drunk tonight"
joke at your Seder?

*

4/20

There's really not much difference between a sweet Jew fro and some natty dreads.

*

EARTH DAY

Jewish grandmothers are the original environmentalists – no piece of wrapping paper goes unrecycled.

*

CINCO DE MAYO

Go easy on the nacho cheese today. You know what it does to you.

*

MOTHER'S DAY

Call your mother (before she calls you).

*

MEMORIAL DAY

Don't you dare put ketchup on that Hebrew National.

*

FATHER'S DAY

Give your dad the best gift ever.
Take your mother out for the day.

*

JULY 4th

If you can make it through the barbecue at your
in-laws without screaming at each other,
it will indeed be a happy 4th of July.

*

Your Mom wanted us to remind you not to
play with matches and/or fireworks.
You'll burn down the house and/or lose a finger.

*

HIGH HOLIDAYS

We're guessing it was a Jewish woman who decided
that the shofar could only be blown two days a year.

*

Our shofar blower used to tour with Springsteen.

*

Tonight we're gonna party like it's 5799!

*

Is it wrong that I got my High Holiday
tickets off StubHub?

*

In preparation for spending time with family over the
holidays, start filling out your list of complaints now.

*

Get all your last minute sinning done this weekend.

*

Pre-ordering for High Holiday
tickets starts online today.
Use the codeword: Atonement.

*

Has anybody seen my good tallis?

*

Get your honey now before they
jack up the prices next week.

*

Right about now, non-Jews around the world are
wondering why they can't find brisket anywhere.

*

Start practicing for next month's atonement.
Skip lunch today.

*

For those of you who have developed a sudden
interest in astronomy, tomorrow's sunset
is at 6:49pm EDT.

*

Fun fact: The Yom Kippur fast never ends
for Jews on the North Pole.

*

Its one shining moment complete, the coffee
percolator goes back into the closet until next year.

*

SUKKOT

After New Year's and Atonement, it's really hard to convince the boss to grant another day off for backyard hut construction.

*

COLUMBUS DAY

A Jewish explorer never would have gotten lost looking for Asian cuisine.

*

HALLOWEEN

Dress as a Jewish mother for Halloween.
It won't do much for the kids, but it'll scare the crap out of the adults.

*

Woke up early to get in line at Walgreen's for the post-Halloween candy sale.

*

THANKSGIVING

Thursday: Macy's Thanksgiving Day Parade.
Friday: Fortunoff's Chanukah Procession.

*

Remember, no matter how crazy it gets during the
meal, they're your family and you love them.

*

Thanksgiving is the one occasion that everyone
in America eats at the same time
most older Jews do every day.

*

CHANUKAH

If the Peanuts had made a Chanukah special,
it would've been called
"You're A Complete Failure, Charlie Brown."

*

Spin the dreidel.
Not nearly as much fun as spin the bottle.

*

It's Day 6. We've officially reached the
"new socks and underwear" portion of Chanukah.

*

Nothing like eight days of gifts to replenish the old
wrapping paper supply.

*

The CEO of Dunkin' Donuts must be shocked by the
spike in jelly category sales this week.

*

You're gonna need a jackhammer to get last year's
wax out of the menorah.

*

CHRISTMAS

The best thing about being Jewish at Christmas
is not having to clean pine needles
off your living room carpet.

*

Oh, holy niiiiight…the flame of the pu-pu platter is
brightly shiiiiining.

*

Why exchange holiday cards when you can
exchange insults instead?

*

If you're looking for something fun to do over the
next two weeks, drive by the mall and watch people
fight for parking spaces.

*

Pop Culture

I'll tell you one thing about
"The Girl with the Dragon Tattoo".
She ain't a Member of the Tribe.

*

Those Dead Sea Spa kiosks at the mall do more to fan
the flames of anti-Semitism than just about
anything else in the world.

*

The one song that hits a little too close
to home for Jewish men:
"Mother" by Pink Floyd.

*

We've always wondered why Klezmer music
wasn't more popular.
Oh, that's right, because it's horrible.

*

While nobody is saying that only Jews should win the Oscars, it's becoming clear that only Jews should host them.

*

Of all the Canadian Jewish rock stars, Geddy Lee is my favorite.

*

When the Black Eyed Peas used the phrase "Mazel Tov" in a song, hip hop died a little bit.

*

Cancelled: Christina Aguilera's scheduled appearance at the Maccabiah Games to sing the Israeli National Anthem.

*

In *Black Swan*, Natalie Portman plays a ballerina driven to madness by an overbearing mother. Not exactly a big stretch for a Jewish girl.

*

Turns out I'm a Cancer, not a Leo.
And all these years I thought I was pushy and
argumentative because I was Jewish.

*

True Grit is a remarkable story
about a courageous girl.
Even more remarkable is that two
Jewish directors made a successful Western.

*

Despite the thousands of new ways to lose weight,
my mom's Tab and Cigarette Diet
from 1977 still seems the most effective.

*

Another couple of movies with Stiller, Hoffman &
Streisand and Robert De Niro will be ready
for his Bar-Mitzvah.

*

I'm psyched for the enhanced pat-downs
at the airport.
After all, I never got that far with most of my
high school dates.

*

Looking forward to seeing the new
Harry Potter movie.
Just can't decide between Christmas Eve
and Christmas Day.

*

You will disappoint someone today.
(Jewish astrology)

*

"A tree has been planted in Israel…"
is the Jewish equivalent of
"A donation has been made in your name…"

*

It's Cyber Monday, which means your mother has
accidentally ordered 14 copies of Danielle Steele's
new book from Amazon.com.

*

Give a Jewish guy a microphone
and he becomes Jerry Seinfeld.
Give him a Casio keyboard
and he becomes Neil Diamond.

*

We're tired of running Hollywood.
Let the Episcopalians do it for a while.

*

Being on crystal meth doesn't explain how
Andre Agassi won all those matches.
But, it does explain how he dated Barbra Streisand.

*

Him: What r u wearing?
Her: A shawl.
Him: That is soooo practical.
(Jewish sexting)

*

I wanted to do a TV show about Shabbos candles,
but "Friday Night Lights" was already taken.

*

There's a Jewish version of
"Eat, Pray, Love." coming out.
It's called "Eat, Pray, Eat Again."

*

The "You Must Be This Tall To Ride" sign:
ruining amusement parks for Jewish kids since 1957.

*

Now that she's single,
is there any chance Mila Kunis
will put a profile up on J-Date?

*

Adam Sandler and Ben Stiller are no
Dustin Hoffman and Richard Dreyfuss.

*

Nobody really knows what Bob Dylan
does or doesn't believe in, but we're still
taking credit for him anyway.

*

Are You Jewish?

You can tell a man is Jewish if he's circumcised.
You can tell a woman is Jewish
if she plays mah-jongg.

*

The Eskimos have over 100 words for "snow."
The Jews have over 100 words for "complain."

*

You'll rarely meet a Jewish alcoholic.
Jews prefer to get addicted to prescription meds:
doctor-approved and covered by insurance.

*

The teen tour: the first and last time a Jew
will travel anywhere by bus.

*

Try as they might, our non-Jewish friends will never
be able to pronounce "chutzpah" correctly.

*

Snow: The 11th Plague.

*

Here's a joke: Two rabbis walk into a bar...
Wait a minute, that would never happen.

*

On my resume, under Special Skills, it says:
Can achieve 5 o'clock shadow by 10:30am,
11 at the latest.

*

Finally got the chance to bust out my new
2011 Complaint-A-Day calendar this weekend.

*

Election Day is bittersweet.
On one hand, the races are finally decided.
On the other hand, we need to find something else
to argue about.

*

This week, the trees are at peak color and
my sinuses are at peak inflammation.

*

Don't criticize self-hating Jews.
Like the rest of us they're just trying to
cut out the middle man.

*

Jews aren't that uptight about pre-marital sex.
Especially since there's no post-marital sex.

*

The schvitz.
Where Jewish men go to let it all hang out.

*

You know fall is coming when you start seeing all
those ads for Back-to-Hebrew-School Sales.

*

I couldn't be an Orthodox rabbi because
I'm not devout enough.
I couldn't be a Reform rabbi because
I don't play guitar.

*

The next big decision facing the Supreme Court:
where to get Chinese food on Christmas Eve.

*

Some Jews go to temple on Saturday mornings.
The rest go to garage sales.

*

Look, after all those years of wandering in the desert
we deserve a little A/C.

*

Sun block is now available in SPF-20, SPF-50 and
SPF-Rabbinical Student.

*

You went to Brandeis? Do you know David Cohen?

*

Everybody complains that the Jews run Hollywood,
but nobody seems to care that we also run
the summer camp industry.

*

This graduation season thousands of Jewish kids will
get the present they never dreamed of:
their grandmother's old car.

*

We don't know for sure, but we bet that a Jew
invented separate temperature controls for the car.

*

A message to our entire Montana fan base:
How ya doin', Larry?

*

A Jewish full house:
yarmulkes from five different family-related events
in your tallis bag.

*

There's no evidence that "Jew's Harp" is an anti-
Semitic name, but we're still slightly offended.

*

You should be so lucky.

*

Jewish women didn't invent the concept of
hyphenating their last names. They just perfected it.

*

Yiddish isn't a real language.
It's just a way for Jews to curse in public.

*

This, I don't need.

*

It's not true that all Jews are Democrats.
Some are Socialists.

*

Your grandmother will send you a birthday card with
a $5 bill in it every year until you reach your mid-40s.

*

Our parents always complained how they grew up in
neighborhoods with strict boundaries.
Then they retired to gated communities.

*

Complaining is an art form.
The only way to master it is to practice constantly.

*

I come from a manufacturing background.
My mother was a matchmaker and my father
was a bookmaker.

*

In airports all across the nation, Jewish travelers are
gathering in hopes of being bumped in exchange
for a free flight.

*

Time to threaten to switch cable companies again so
we can get three free months of movie channels.

*

Complimentary jelly packets from restaurants
can be given to small children as gifts.
They don't know any better.

*

If you don't see the tip jar, it doesn't exist.

*

Would it kill the supermarket to give us a little
advance notice on the free sample days?

*

Every Jewish woman longs to hear those
three little words:
No purchase necessary.

*

For you, almost free.

*

Suckers pay retail.

*

A half-price, mediocre dinner at 4:30pm beats
a full-price, excellent dinner at 7pm any day.

*

Everything tastes better when it's free.

*

Most people get fake IDs so they can get into bars.
Jews get fake IDs so they can get the
senior citizen discount.

*

The two scariest words for any Jew at a restaurant:
coat check.

*

You could buy that now at full price.
Or, you could wait until it's on sale at Marshall's.

*

Sugar and jelly packets are complimentary –
feel free to take as many as you want.

*

Did you check to see if there's a coupon for that
in the Entertainment book?

*

Your grandparents' condo and The Elbo Room:
They're both in Ft. Lauderdale,
but they're worlds apart.

*

Jews don't believe in hell.
After all, nothing could be worse than Florida
in the summer.

*

Many flights to Honolulu from the East Coast
run through Dallas.
It's the only time most Jews ever see Texas.

*

The capital of Israel is Jerusalem.
The capital of America is Brooklyn.

*

PART 2: CHAI-KUS

Japanese poetry about people who love Chinese food

Bagel with a schmear.
A brunch's finest moment.
Tragedy! No lox.

*

Polo shirt, collar
up. Reeking of Drakkar Noir.
U.S.Y. Dance King.

*

Double cheese pizza.
Me? Lactose intolerant.
Soy milk anyone?

*

JCC hoop team.
Sunday mornings on the court.
Our center, 5'-9".

*

*Yom Kippur fasting
wouldn't be so bad, except
for Sara Lee ads.*

*

*Harvard undergrad.
Masters from Columbia.
Still living at home.*

*

*Winters in Boca.
Summers at the Jersey Shore.
Christmas in Vegas.*

*

*Got a runny nose?
No need to worry. Mom has
tissues in her sleeve.*

*

Fantasy football,
Fantasy baseball and golf.
Jewish exercise.

*

Matzo: Flour and water.
The same ingredients that
they use to make paste.

*

Still don't get why Jews
can't get tattoos but can get
plastic surgery.

*

Curse your Siren song!
So lovely...so tempting...so
forbidden. Bacon.

*

"Your mother just called.
She's on her way over now."
Scariest words yet.

*

The Chinese buffet.
Where two mismatched cultures bond
over boneless ribs.

*

My Bubbie always said
I was a genius. Still haven't
convinced my parents.

*

Is it wrong to check
out women while the rabbi
speaks of atonement?

*

How many goldfish
die before PETA storms a
Purim Carnival?

*

Music, movies, books.
Enough already. You win,
Ms. Barbra Streisand.

*

Kosher dill pickles.
Great when fresh. Even better when
free at the deli.

*

Like my sports heroes
I will not coach youth soccer
on Rosh Hashanah.

*

*Buck Dharma is a
much cooler rock 'n' roll name
than Donald Roeser.*

*

*My parents call to
see if everything's all right
and tell me what's wrong.*

*

*My best friend felt good.
Then, he felt really guilty
and felt much better.*

*

*Oddly, there's lots of
Jewish heavy metal stars.
Keppe-bangers, no?*

*

*I'm sorry, but the
Lender's Bagel people can't
really be Jewish.*

*

*My Bubbie only
spoke Yiddish when she wanted
to yell at my dad.*

*

*I'm afraid that my
daughter's Bat-Mitzvah will cost
more than my wedding.*

*

*Jewish sports stars: Few.
And yet, the list of Jewish
sportswriters: Epic.*

*

The groom: Ben Perlman.
The bride: Leah Kane-Feinstein-
Schwartz-Goldblum-Perlman.

*

Wearing a large gold
Chai will bring you lots of luck.
Just not with women.

*

Peter Criss is the
only non-Jew in Kiss. But,
he did yearn for Beth.

*

Rhinoplasty: From
the ancient Hebrew meaning:
A Bat-Mitzvah gift.

*

*'Tis better to love
someone your parents hate than
not to love at all.*

*

*There are no Jewish
ghosts. We prefer to do our
haunting in real life.*

*

*Jewish girls can't be
strippers. When you give them cash,
they just buy more clothes.*

*

*We make some of the
best food in the world. Why can't
we solve chocolate?*

*

*Jews used to own the
basketball court. Now, we just
own all of the teams.*

*

*Burning bushes? Yes.
Parting seas? Sure. Tornados?
Not where I come from.*

*

*Mother moving in?
On the bright side, think what you'll
save on birth control.*

*

*Become a lawyer?
Too cliché. I went into
comedy instead.*

*

*Bagel, sausage and
cheddar. If I'm going down,
I'm going down hard.*

*

*To get laid, some guys
go into music. Jewish
guys become doctors.*

*

*If I confessed all
of my sins each week, I'd have
time for little else.*

*

*Adam Duritz slept
with Courtney and Jen. Hello
Lantzman Hall-of-Fame!*

*

*If I wanted all
this heat and damp, I'd move to
Florida sooner.*

*

*Dunkin' Donuts gets
their bagels from Pillsbury.
Well, that explains it.*

*

*LeBron left Cleveland
for Miami. He went from
cold Jews to old Jews.*

*

*Is "Dinner for Schmucks"
a Steve Carell flick or a
meal with my brother?*

*

I grew a goatee
to seem tough, but just looked like
a rebel Hasid.

*

"No lox," said the guy.
"Smoked salmon?" I asked in jest.
"That, we got," he said.

*

Funny. Red Sox fans
sing Neil Diamond while Yanks fans
go Irish tenor.

*

Orthodox, reform
and conservative: The three
faiths on a teen tour.

*

My max bench press is
two-fifty. Or three of my
Bubbie's matzo balls.

*

Fight high blood pressure.
Diet, exercise and don't
take your mother's calls.

*

Justices Kagan,
Bader-Ginsburg and Breyer.
Need one more for bridge.

*

If Chicago is
called "Chi-town," shouldn't New York
be known as "Chai-town?"

*

*Can't wait for the Nets
to move to Brooklyn. Vendors
selling hot knishes.*

*

*Dad hates when we treat.
Missing the senior discount
just about kills him.*

*

*Fiddler on the Roof.
"Get down from there!" yelled my mom.
"You'll break your damn neck!"*

*

*At the Jersey Shore.
Spent 40 bucks on games. Won
10 cents worth of crap.*

*

*Every grandchild has
vacationed at Florida's
Century Village.*

*

*My daughter got her
Bat-Mitzvah date last weekend.
She's ten, for Pete's sake!*

*

*My folks are married
47 years. Time to
start planning the cruise.*

*

*Hillel House. The one
place where Jewish parents hope
their kids will hook up.*

*

Apples and honey.
Brisket, matzo balls and wine.
Rolaids and Pepto.

*

Had trouble getting
tickets for temple this year.
Scalpers were brutal.

*

My tallis bag is
a vault for parking passes
of holidays past.

*

Family is nice
when well-fed. Yom Kippur is
a different story.

*

*Ambitious Gentiles
could make a fortune at shul
by valet parking.*

*

*Worried that ten days
might be insufficient to
cover this year's sins.*

*

*The circumcision.
Painful custom followed by
deli sandwiches.*

*

*If I plant one more
tree in Israel, they'll call it
The Negev Forest.*

*

Dylan is unique.
He's the only famous Jew
from Minnesota.

*

Early Chanukah
this year. Chocolate gelt will
be slightly less stale.

*

Our parents quote Berle.
We quote Seinfeld. And our kids
will quote Jon Stewart.

*

When Number 20
steps to the plate, are the fans
yelling "Youuuuuk" or "Jewwwww?"

*

Would buying a drink
for someone in a saloon
be a "bar" mitzvah?

*

You take a few beets,
squish them and top with sour cream?
Borscht. I don't get it.

*

Jujubes, Juicy
Fruit, JujyFruits. Jews run the
candy industry.

*

Harvard, Yale, Princeton.
The only schools grandparents
have ever heard of.

*

"Can I have pickles?"
"Not until you order, dear."
The deli teaser.

*

Mogen David wine.
It's the Night Train Express of
Jewish alcohol.

*

Went as a hobo.
"Wear the clothes you always do,"
taunted my mother.

*

Does my UNICEF
donation qualify as
a tax deduction?

*

Overprotective?
Wouldn't even let me dress
as a football star.

*

Hard to look scary
with a winter coat over
your zombie costume.

*

Opportunity
for sabras to dress slutty?
Halloween parties.

*

Each November 1st,
Dr. Schwartz hits the jackpot.
He's the town dentist.

*

My cousin Sheila
is pretty hot. Still not an
ideal prom date, though.

*

Went to Israel. Saw
soldiers with guns. But, I got
shot down by the girls.

*

Shampoos and rinses,
conditioners and mousses
can't tame the Jew 'fro.

*

Diamond, Horowitz
and Yauch. Manhattan law firm?
No. The Beastie Boys.

*

*At twenty, you're told
"Marry Jewish." At forty,
you're told "Just marry!"*

*

*Can't mix milk and beef.
But, why not milk and chicken?
Chickens don't lactate.*

*

*We should drop the ball
for the Jewish New Year. It's
warm in Times Square then.*

*

*Forget line dances,
step dances and square dances.
I'll rock the Hora.*

*

Commandment Number
Eleven: Thou shalt go to
a sleep-away camp.

*

When I taste beef tongue
I always get the feeling
it's tasting me back.

*

Jewish mothers would
pass laws that required helmets
even while you slept.

*

Forget the Rogaine.
Try to get your body hair
to migrate northward.

*

*Diamonds are a girl's
best friend. But, she's real tight with
gold and silver too.*

*

*When my kids are bad,
they don't go to their rooms. They
go to my parents.*

*

*Superman should have
a Jewish counterpart. We'll
call him Silverman.*

*

*Our parents went from
always wrong to always right
back to always wrong.*

*

*I saw a Jewish
porno the other day. It
was called "Deep Regret."*

*

*We're bad at soccer.
No way can eleven Jews
agree on one goal.*

*

*If you are feeling
happy and optimistic,
don't worry. It'll pass.*

*

*Love may be fleeting,
but petty grudges and ill will
can last forever.*

*

*My friend is afraid
to eat kishke. Clearly, he
doesn't have the guts.*

*

*If diamonds are
forever, then how come the
oral sex isn't?*

*

*J-Date would have come
sooner, but our moms couldn't
work the computer.*

*

*During the Hora,
I'm the guy who has to lift
the overweight uncle.*

*

PART 3: ESSAYS

We wish we were making this stuff up

Guide to Jews

Agnostic (Cultural) Jews

The first mistake people make when considering Jews is in thinking of Judaism as merely a religion. Yes, Judaism is a very old religion – so old in fact that there's plenty of animal sacrificin' fun in the texts. But many, many Jews are not religious in the least bit and yet they still consider themselves to be Jewish. You see, Judaism is a culture as well as a religion. You don't have to be down with Yahweh to be down from your mother's relentless nagging! Jewish culture includes things like salty delicatessen foods, sleep-away camps, teen tours, expectations that you'll be a doctor or a lawyer, using Yiddish swears and inexplicably rooting for any celebrity Jew, no matter how lame (e.g. Dee Snider).

By the way, a Jew is generally defined as anyone who has at least one Jewish grandparent or is a convert to Judaism (can't lose Sammy from the list!) Sorry, Madge, but modern Kabbalah adherents don't count.

Religious Jews

Like salsa, religious Jews come in 3 basic flavors: mild, medium and hot.

Reform (mild) Jews are a little more easygoing about the religious laws they wish to follow. As long as you publicly declare allegiance to the God of Moses (and privately consider yourself one of the 'chosen people') then you're in. Reform services are mostly in

English, guitars are often featured, and women are allowed to lead. These are the liberal religious Jews.

Conservative (medium) Jews are devout enough to separate themselves from the Reformers without having to go all the way to 11. The big differences are that Conservatives have services largely in Hebrew, make a huge deal about the High Holidays and get really mad when you marry hot Irish babes.

Orthodox (hot) Jews don't mess around. Not only do they celebrate all of the major holidays, but they also celebrate the minor holidays (e.g. Purim, Tu B'Shevat) and observe the Sabbath. That means services and candle lighting every Friday night and restricted activities on Saturday. Services are completely in Hebrew. If you have to ask, you're in the wrong shul, boychik.

Finally, to clear up one important matter: Yes, it's true that Jews sell tickets to temple for the High Holidays (Rosh Hashanah and Yom Kippur). We know that many non-Jews find this to be gauche, but it's not. Think of it like the NPR annual fund drive – Jews hit you up for the big check once a year rather than going for the five or ten spot every week. And obviously you're going to hold the fund drive on the biggest day of the year.

Tough Jews

Now by "Tough Jews" we don't mean sports-tough Jews like Jay Fiedler or Gabe Kapler. We mean crazy, gun-toting, ready to rumble Jews. Roughly half of the Jews in the world live in Israel and by law they all serve a stint in the tough-as-nails Israeli Army when they turn 18. Obviously the combination of the fighty Middle East environment and the military training toughens them up considerably, especially compared to their wimpy US cousins. Now, we've been to Israel (summer on the kibbutz, baby!) and we can assure you that it's full of the toughest Jews you'll ever meet. Here in America we generally don't think of Jews as being thuggy gangsters (well, maybe Meyer Lansky) but they're out there and all of us have the hidden potential. You've been warned!

Funny Jews

The list of funny Jews is endless. Funny Jews are our people's bread and butter. We would assert – all obvious biases aside – that Jews are by and large the funniest ethnic group in the world. Richard Lewis. Ben Stiller. Jon Lovitz. Woody Allen. Jerry Seinfeld. Jerry Lewis. Bronson Pinchot. Jon Stewart. Rodney Dangerfield. The list goes on and on. We've got low-brow, high-brow, intellectual, political, physical, you name it – every kind of humor is well-represented by the House of (Larry) David.

No one really knows how Jews came to be so funny. We suspect that it developed as a defense mechanism to compensate for our poor athletic skills. But Jews ARE funny. If you don't believe us, try to find a successful sitcom without one.

Hot Jews

There are more hot Jews in the world than you might realize. And we're not just talking Mandy Patinkin hot. We're talking Natalie Portman, Rachel Weisz and Mila Kunis hot!

Christmas Jews

Another common misconception is that Jews don't like Christmas. Not true! We like it just fine. It's just not that big a deal to us. A typical Jewish Christmas involves Chinese food and a movie. Sure, it sucks that we don't get a Rankin/Bass Hanukkah special, and everybody hates that stupid Adam Sandler song, but what are you going to do? By and large, Jews enjoy Christmas just like everybody else.

Summary

As you can see from our exhaustive research, Jews can't be lumped into one monolithic group – there's at least sixolithic groups! Jews are just like everybody else in the world – some are good, some are bad, some are cool and some are annoying. So, please, don't blame all of us for Joe Lieberman.

*

The Name Game

There are many famous actors, politicians, athletes and other public figures whose names suggest that they might be Members of the Tribe (M.O.T.). And while it's fun to speculate who is and who isn't, we here at Jews Clues decided it was time for some definitive answers. That's why our crackerjack staff has put together a list of people who have the nom, but not the Yom.

Bruce Springsteen (Musician): All signs point to Jewish: the name, the New Jersey upbringing, the power to grow a beard overnight. It's his ability to dance that gives him away, however.

Julius Irving (Hall-of-Fame Basketball Player): He might be a Doctor, but come on...the guy can dunk!

Philip Seymour Hoffman (Actor): Never has one man had so many Jewish-sounding names, yet been so profoundly non-Jewish.

Steven Segal ("Actor"/Lawman): No Jew has ever kicked butt like that. Ever.

David Cone (Pitcher, New York Mets): Completely comfortable pitching on the High Holidays.

Torah Bright (Australian Snowboard Champion): Perhaps she was conceived after her parents attended a neighbor's Chanukah party?

W. Axl Rose (Lead Singer, Guns 'n' Roses): Leather pants, tattoos, straight hair…seriously?

Stephanie Seymour (Supermodel): What sane Jewish girl would date Axl Rose?

Lou Diamond Philips (Actor): Maybe if 'La Bamba' had been 'La Hora'…

Ron Howard (Actor/Director): Playing white-bread, Midwestern teenager Richie Cunningham was not a stretch.

Malcolm Young (Rhythm Guitarist, AC/DC): Although his dirty deeds were done dirt cheap.

Albus Dumbledore (Headmaster, Hogwarts School of Witchcraft and Wizardry): The beard works, but the robe has got to go.

Jeff Gordon (NASCAR driver): No way would his mother ever let him get behind the wheel of that rocket ship.

*

The Beets of Wrath

As a six-year-old, I worshiped the Six Million Dollar Man. Colonel Steve Austin was everything you could want in a hero. He was strong, he was fast, he was part robot, he had his own theme music and his parents let him wear that nifty red sweat suit every day. Oh, and by the way, he was a former freakin' astronaut to boot. The guy had it all.

My brother Dan, who was four at the time, was also a fan. (Although Col. Austin paled in comparison to The Incredible Hulk in his estimation.) He and I would incorporate the adventures of the "Bionic Man" into our own playtime. We would run so fast that we were sure people watching us could only see a blur of arms and legs. And when we jumped, we would make Steve's trademark sound that accompanied each of his slow motion leaps. Ba-na-na-na-na-na-na-na. In our heads, we were broad-jumping to the top of 10-foot walls or hurtling barbed wire fences. In reality, we were doing very slow deep knee bends and soaring over extremely small rocks or, in a best-case scenario, our sleeping dog Bo.

Every Friday night, I religiously parked myself in front of the TV and watched Steve take on a variety of domestic and foreign bad guys. Of course, he hardly ever killed anybody because nobody really died in 70's action television. (Only in sitcoms.) Then, when they introduced The Bionic Woman, played by Disco-era super fox Lindsay Wagner (now hawking mattresses on late night TV), it was almost more than my pre-pubescent psyche could handle.

Watching Steve and Jaime Sommers team up to foil some international spy ring while flirting shamelessly with each other proved to be the perfect cocktail of sanitized combat and sex.

Steve, with his way-cool bionic arm, leg and eye and Jaime with her bionic ear. Really? A bionic ear? Cue Comic Book Guy: Worst. Bionic. Power. Ever. Jaime's enhanced aural capacities gave her the ability to overhear conversations that were taking place between 20 and 100 feet from where she stood. This power is only valuable if you're a teenage girl and you want to know if your friends are calling you a slut behind your back. Otherwise, it's pretty fucking useless.

That didn't matter to me, though. Steve Austin was awesome enough for the both of them. And it would have taken a natural disaster or an ill-timed Test of the Emergency Broadcast System for me to miss a single minute of the show. As it turned out, it was neither of these things that led to the one and only time I failed to keep my weekly date with Col. Austin. Instead, it was a plate of cooked beets.

Like many children, Dan and I were fussy eaters. All we ever wanted was hamburgers and spaghetti. Preferably, both at the same time. We turned our noses up at nearly every vegetable save the occasional corn-on-the-cob. And only if it was smeared with butter. To the best of my recollection, I didn't put anything green and leafy into my mouth until I was in junior high school.

My mother tried everything to get us to eat new (and healthy) things. She hid vegetables in the spaghetti sauce, she fried them, she dipped them in cheese. I think, at one point, she even offered cash incentives for finishing a handful of peas. But Dan and I fought her every step of the way. Knowing us, we were probably miserable little bastards about the whole thing too. We'd hide vegetables under mashed potatoes or squish them up in our napkins or push them onto the floor where Bo would eat them. Whatever tactic my mother tried, we parried with a counterattack. It must've been infuriating.

One night, it all came to a head. The plates that my mother brought to the table for Dan and me that fateful evening contained a hamburger and a pile of slimy-looking puce discs. When we looked at her quizzically, she said, "Those are beets. They're delicious. Take a no-thank-you helping."

A "no-thank-you" helping was my mother's way of telling us to try a mouthful of something. She didn't expect us to finish it. She just wanted us to try it. And yet, every time she told us to take a no-thank-you-helping we had the same wiseass response as we did on the night she put those beets in front of us.

"No thank you," we both chirped simultaneously.

Only this time, my father stepped in.

"Enough!" he boomed, slamming both hands down on the table and rattling the flatware. "You guys are gonna try those beets if it kills you."

"But, Dad…" I started to protest.

"No buts, CJ," he said, cutting me off. "You're the big brother. You try them first and show Danny they're okay."

I glanced over at Dan. His lower lip had begun to quiver slightly and he looked at me expectantly. The beets lay before me, slightly cooler now and significantly less appetizing. I picked one up on my fork and studied it. Maybe it wouldn't be so bad. Maybe it would be like cranberry sauce. After all, it was the same shape and color. Maybe the taste was similar as well.

Moving the fork to my lips, I opened my mouth and let the innocuous root vegetable slide in. The initial flavor was earthy, kind of like getting a mouthful of dirt. A little gross, but not horrible. Then, as I began to chew, the beet released its full demonic essence. The juices and flesh of the vegetable combined to create a mélange of gloppy sludge in my mouth that, to my young palate, tasted like unwashed sweat socks.

"Blech! I spat. "This is awful!"

Across the table from me, Dan began to sob.

"If CJ doesn't like it, I don't want to eat it!" he wailed.

My father whirled on me.

"This is your fault! If you hadn't reacted like that, he wouldn't be crying. He'd better eat one of those beets or YOU CAN'T WATCH THE SIX MILLION DOLLAR MAN!"

When the last of those words bounced off the walls of our dining room, my arms and legs turned to jelly as my entire mental capacity was focused on processing the decree my father had just issued.

Not watch The Six Million Dollar Man? But, that was impossible. You might as well tell me I couldn't breathe air. Or that ice cream was now illegal. Or that the Red Sox were moving to Albany.

Not watch The Six Million Dollar Man? No! I could not allow this to happen. Come on, CJ! Think, dammit!

"Dan," I said in my most placating voice, "you can eat the beet. I was just kidding. It's not that bad."

"You're lying!" screamed Dan, verging on the edge of hysteria.

"No, no. I'm not. Look, I'll eat another one."

Taking a deep breath, I picked up a beet with my fingers and shoved it into my mouth. After a few cursory chews, I swallowed before my taste buds realized what was happening.

"See," I said with what I hoped was a winning smile.

Tears continued to roll down Dan's cheeks, but he was no longer bawling. He contemplated the beets on his plate before picking up the smallest one in the pile.

"Go ahead," I urged. "You can do it."

Looking first at me and then at my parents, Dan moved the beet in Bionic Man-like slow motion toward his lips. I could almost hear the Ba-na-na-na-na-na-na-na in my head. He parted his teeth ever so slightly and placed the beet on his tongue. Then, his mouth closed. It was in.

I almost thought he was going to make it. In my mind, he would chew it a couple times, swallow and make a face to show that he didn't like it but had at least tried it. Then, we could put this whole regrettable incident behind us and I could remain faithful to Steve and Jaime.

But, that's not how it worked out.

Upon taking a bite of the selected beet, Dan reacted as if he just eaten a handful of worms.

"I doan yike it!" he said around the contents of his mouth.

"He's gotta swallow it or there's no Bionic Man!" bellowed my father.

Now I began to cry.

"Come on, Dan." I begged. "Just swallow it. I'll give you all my toys. Whatever you want. Just swallow."

Fresh tears sprang to Dan's eyes as he opened his mouth and allowed purple liquid and semi-solid pieces of beet to drip down his chin and onto his white t-shirt. In that half-chewed mess, I could see The Six Million Dollar Man slipping away.

The combination of watching the slime ooze over Dan's lips and realizing that my Friday night TV time was doomed became too overwhelming for me. Without warning, I turned and threw up on the dining room floor.

Dan, seeing me toss my cookies and still having a good deal of beet in his mouth, began to gag. My mother, who had started toward me to help, quickly veered to her right, grabbed Dan and hustled him to a nearby bathroom where he emptied his stomach into an unsuspecting toilet bowl.

My father stood up and surveyed the scene: His oldest son was lying on the floor moaning next to a sizeable puddle of vomit. His youngest son was retching over the porcelain throne. And various chunks of beet lay scattered about the room. Thinking quickly, he went upstairs, turned on the TV and pretended that nothing out of the ordinary had occurred at dinner that night.

As I lay in the darkness of my room the following Friday night while Col. Austin battled the forces of badness under the admiring gaze of millions of children who had not been punished, I thought ruefully about the injustice of my situation.

"This sucks." I whispered aloud to nobody. Although, in the back of my mind, I wondered if Jaime Sommers could hear me.

*

A Yarmulke Named Eric

Some of my oldest and dearest friends date back to my first year of Hebrew School at Temple Aliyah. As we sat in Mrs. Rosenberg's classroom trying to learn our aleph-bets and our Jewish history, we formed bonds and shared jokes that still connect us over 30 years later.

My friend Eric and I still talk about our adventures as restless 8-year-olds doing our best to appear attentive while still goofing off at the same time. While Eric is one of the most responsible adults I know, as a kid he was always pushing the buttons of the authority figures that governed us. If the teacher turned her back and a book dropped, it was most likely Eric. If the sounds of artificial flatulence came from the back of the class, Eric was probably the source. If a kid suddenly found himself with a damp auditory canal, Eric had no doubt applied the Wet Willie.

As a result of his antics, Eric was forever being banished from our classroom. There was an unused office right outside the door that served as the penalty box for unruly students. Since Eric was a frequent visitor to this office, he developed a good working knowledge of its contents and how they could be used for further subversion. One such weapon of mass distraction was an office chair that had somehow lost its back, rendering it little more than an ottoman on wheels. But, where others merely saw damaged furniture Eric saw opportunity.

Stepping quietly out of the office, Eric dragged the

chair to the far end of the empty hallway and then prepared for takeoff. Running with the chair until he reached maximum velocity, he then flung himself onto the seat and rolled the rest of the way down the hallway until he crashed into Mrs. Rosenberg's closed door. The resounding thud shook the classroom and dissolved us all into giggles that quickly became hysteria when Mrs. Rosenberg opened the door and found Eric and the chair in a tangled heap at her feet.

While Mrs. Rosenberg barely tolerated Eric's antics, there was something else that he did (or failed to do) by which she could not abide. On the first day of class, we were given the assignment of finding out our Hebrew names. Mrs. Rosenberg would then write that name, in Hebrew, with a Sharpie on a new white yarmulke. This would become the yarmulke that we'd wear in class every day. At the next class a few days later everyone came in with their Hebrew names written on a piece of notebook paper. Except for Eric.

Going from student to student, Mrs. Rosenberg dutifully recorded all the Moshes and Rivkas and Yakovs and Leahs. Until she got to Eric.

"And did you find out what is your Hebrew name, Eric?" she asked in her slight Russian accent.

"Um," replied Eric. "My parents are looking into it."

"Vell, see that you have it next time," she warned.

The next class came and we all sat in a large semi-circle with our newly personalized yarmulkes. All that is, except for Eric, who sported a blindingly white and conspicuously unmarked skullcap.

"Did your parents find out your Hebrew name?" inquired Mrs. Rosenberg of Eric.

"They're checking with my grandparents," responded Eric.

"I see," replied Mrs. Rosenberg dubiously. "Perhaps you vill haf it next time?"

"Absolutely," chirped Eric with a winning smile.

The next class brought a different excuse-"My grandparents think it was lost on the boat from Russia. They're checking with my great uncle."

The class after that, still another-"They think there's a rabbi in eastern Europe who has it. They're trying to track him down."

As the year wore on, the excuses became more and more creative.

"A dog ate it."

"We had it, but my sister destroyed it because I ripped her David Cassidy poster."

"Aliens stole it from me when I was an infant."

Finally, Mrs. Rosenberg took Eric's yarmulke from him at the end of class one day. The next time we convened, she gave it to him with mock formality.

"I am pleased to present you with your yarmulke," she intoned, bowing slightly.

Eric took it, looked at it briefly, and put it on his head. There, in clear block letters that bespoke more than a little frustration was a name:

ERIC

From then on, whenever she did roll call at the beginning of the class, Mrs. Rosenberg would work her way down the attendance list in Hebrew:

"...Yitzhak

Freidl

Yosef

Berylah

Rachmiel...

And then, pausing meaningfully, she would look at the yarmulke mocking her from the top of my friend's head.

...and ERIC!" she would finish, spitting the name like venom at the smirking class.

Eric would merely shrug, raise his hand, and say, "Here."

I think about Mrs. Rosenberg every so often and hope that she had more obedient and conscientious students after us. Or, at the very least, that they got rid of the broken chair in the office next to her class.

*

Rhapsody in Powder Blue

When John Travolta donned his famous white suit in Saturday Night Fever, he spawned a fashion trend that endured until disco was literally burned at the stake in Comiskey Park one sultry night in July of 1979. Stepping in to fill the giant void in poor taste was the powder blue three-piece suit, a haberdashery disaster whose time (unfortunately) did not come to an end until after my Bar-Mitzvah in 1982.

As I look at the picture of myself standing proudly before the ark with wild, puffy hair, a mouth full of shiny metal and the matching blue pants, jacket and vest whose best feature was the fact that it was fire resistant, I wonder how I wasn't laughed off the bimah. Why would you dress someone who was theoretically becoming a man in an outfit that would get him beaten up in any establishment where actual men hung out?

It was because of this outfit that I was already at a deficit when I began to chant the opening prayers to my Haftorah portion. Being first-born and a perfectionist and slightly OCD, I had practiced my Haftorah twice every day while attending West End House Camp in the summer of '82. By Visiting Day, every kid in my bunk, regardless of religious affiliation, knew my entire Bar-Mitzvah front to back.

I'll never forget the day when one of my Irish bunkmates stopped my daily practice to correct me on my interpretation of a trope in my Maftir. Despite my avid preparation, however, I still could not overcome the bane of many a Bar-Mitzvah boy. My voice was changing.

The blessing before the Haftorah, while linguistically flawless, sounded like two cats fighting in a bag lined with aluminum foil. I glanced over at the cantor, a patient and gentle man, who simply smiled and nodded reassuringly. Forging ahead, I sonically annihilated the remainder of the service while silently giving thanks for our rabbi's ban on recording devices in the synagogue.

The ceremony over and behind me, it was now time to party. And if by party you take me to mean the Oneg Shabbat and luncheon, then clearly you've been to a Saturday morning affair or two. The Kids Party was taking place at the VFW Hall later that night, but the older friends and relatives were being treated to a nice midday meal in the temple function hall.

Perhaps the best part of the luncheon was the open bar. Not many people took advantage of it, but it was there nonetheless. It did afford me the opportunity to score drinks for two pretty girls in my class. I simply told the bartender that the Sombreros were for my mother and aunt. (Things were different then. Kids could order drinks at bars. You could buy cigarettes from machines. Better days.)

When the luncheon ended and the envelopes had been collected, I had only one priority before the party that night. In my junior high school years, the hottest fashion item in town was something called Sweats bi Ebe. They were basically fancy sweatpants with piping on the sides and an elastic waistband. I don't know if the Ebe thing was a national craze or a phenomenon that was isolated here in the Northeast. Looking back, I have no idea why everyone wanted to look like escapees from a geriatric center. Regardless (or irregardless, as we say here), every cool guy had a pair of Sweats bi Ebe at the time and I wanted them.

Somehow I conned my Aunt Sally into taking me to Jordan Marsh in the hours before the party so I could purchase the Ebes for my big moment that night. I found the pair I wanted, blue with red piping, got my super-cool aunt to spot me the cash and walked out of Jordan's with my prize.

Back at home, I peeled off the blue suit that would forever carbon date my Bar-Mitzvah for future archivists and stepped into another item that millions (or at least thousands) would later regret. Did those pants make me any more suave that night? No. I still bumbled around the VFW Hall, barely working up the courage to ask girls to dance in my cracking, off-pitch voice. Did I later spill soda on the treasured Ebes? Perhaps. But, we shan't speak of that because I've blocked most of that memory anyway.

Did I learn anything? Yes.

Three years later when my brother was Bar-Mitzvah'd, I wore something to his party that showed I was no longer a slave to the couture of the moment. Something that showed I was a man of refined and classical taste. Something that, try as they might, my parents couldn't airbrush from the pictures.

I wore parachute pants.

*

My Secret Life as an '80s Radical

Kids have it so easy nowadays. Sure, it's hotter than ever due to global warming but public schools have gone soft. Back in the early 1980s when I was in middle school we had two problems that today's kids would never have to deal with. First, there was no air conditioning in school and second, we weren't allowed to wear shorts.

It was barbaric treatment, to put it mildly, and I think it's high time that people heard the real story of why there's both air conditioning and shorts-wearing in today's schools.

Our tale begins with a plucky young radical from Marlboro, New Jersey. This man-child was the Norma Rae of his generation. This boy fought the law and, for once, the law didn't win. Few know the true story of that boy, but I do.

I know the story because I was that young boy.

It was so very hot at Marlboro Middle School, especially in June and double especially when you had art class with Mr. Sharkey on the third floor. Absent shorts, our pant choices were limited to just two bad options: denim or parachute pants.

No one knows where parachute pants came from or where they've gone. But for a brief period in the Reagan era they were everywhere. The closest modern approximate is workout pants, but imagine if your workout pants: a) didn't breathe; b) were fluorescent colored; and c) were covered in pocket-less zippers. Sound awful? They were. But we had no choice. Parachute pants, rubber bracelets and shoulder pads were in style and we were a docile generation.

You have to understand that things were different back then. Movies like *The Day After Tomorrow* made us fear nuclear war on a daily basis and we were all convinced that Orwell's *1984* was going to come true on the day after the day after tomorrow. We were obedient kids, well trained to do as we were told, always scared of mushroom clouds and cages full of bitey rats.

But it was so hot. And the girls didn't care because they were allowed to wear skirts. We begged the teachers and the principals to let us wear shorts. They declined. We asked our parents to intervene. They demurred. We tried to start a blog rally, but couldn't because the stupid internet wasn't invented yet. Our situation looked hopeless.

Even the soothing sounds of Howard Jones on my Walkman couldn't stop me from obsessing nonstop about the heat. And it was so much worse for me than anyone else in the entire world for I was both chubby and a redhead. I had to take action.

I rallied my male classmates and came up with a crazy solution. If they wouldn't let us wear shorts than we would start wearing skirts to school until they relented! (Actually, we wanted to wear kilts, feeling that they were a more macho option, but none of us knew of any Scottish clothing stores in bicycle range of Marlboro.)

As you can imagine, all hell broke loose on the day that we showed up to school in drag. Bear in mind that this was long before emo kids started wearing skinny jeans and eyeliner. Cross-dressing was strictly forbidden and a source of major embarrassment for any upper-middle class suburban school system.

Unsurprisingly, we were sent home that day and threatened with detention, suspension and reprogramming. But the administration was quickly forced to give in to our demands after the news media got involved. Once *The Asbury Park Press* caught wind of our protest and featured our story on their front page, victory was ours.

In many ways it was the defining moment of my life. A twelve year old boy – not even yet a Bar Mitzvah! – took on the system and won. Ever since that day shorts have been allowed in every school in America, all due to our heroic efforts.

They recently celebrated the 40th anniversary of Woodstock, but what did those hippies ever really accomplish besides deluding themselves that they could think the rain away? We revolutionized everything 27 years ago and you're only hearing the story today. We changed the world, man. Where's my commemorative expanded DVD box set? Where's my limited edition Peter Max poster?

(Legal note: certain aspects of this story may have been slightly altered for entertainment value. The following parts are definitely true: 1) it was really hot at school when I was a kid; 2) I did go to Marlboro Middle School and Mr. Sharkey was my art teacher; 3) I did wear a lot of parachute pants; 4) I did enjoy listening to Howard Jones on my Walkman. The rest may or may not have happened.)

*

Ain't No Party Like A USY Party

When I reached my teenage years and began my long and largely unsuccessful quest of trying to pick-up women, the highlight of every month was the USY dance. USY, or United Synagogues Youth, was the predominant social club for Jewish teens in my area. Some of you may have grown up with AZA or B'nai B'rith or some other youth group, but in my neck of the woods USY was the only game in town. And when there was a USY dance, you didn't miss it.

See, USY dances were the exception to the normal teenage hook-up rules. While most parents and authority figures (and Tipper Gore) were telling you to practice chastity and restraint, the USY dance was the Playboy Mansion Grotto by comparison. Not that people were getting naked under the bleachers, but nobody broke it up if you were making out on the dance floor either.

There was a different aesthetic to the USY dance for the adults in our lives. Sure, we were all still horny teenagers with hormones raging out of control. But, we were all Jewish horny teenagers. And if teenagers were going to do what teenagers do, at least we were doing it with other Jewish kids. As a result, our parents willingly and happily sent us off to these monthly events. And if we had to miss one for some reason, they were even more disappointed than we were.

So we put on our parachute pants, slathered on some Drakkar Noir and did the circuit. Towns like Sharon,

Lexington, Randolph and Peabody were where we made our names. We'd ride into town on a big, yellow school bus, pop the collars of our Polo shirts and prepare to break some hearts.

Striding confidently into the gym (or community room of the host synagogue), the first thing we did was "take a lap," surveying the scene for sabras with scam potential. Then, one of us would work up the courage to ask a girl to dance during a fast song in hopes that a slow dance would come up next allowing us the opportunity for some full body contact. If one of my friends was interested in a girl who was ensconced in a phalanx of other dancing girls we'd break up that protective circle like the Notre Dame Flying Wedge, charging the dance floor en masse and asking the entire group to dance so that our boy could have his shot at the now unguarded female.

If things went well, you'd end up swapping spit and engaging in a little light petting with the object of your desire and then you'd exchange phone numbers. After that came a series of phone calls resulting in a date, usually at some mall that was very inconvenient for your parents to drive you to. My personal record was a rendezvous in Warwick, Rhode Island-a solid hour from where I lived. Suddenly, my parents weren't so enthusiastic anymore. But, hey, at least she was Jewish.

By the time we got our driver's licenses, USY dances had started to lose their appeal. With so many other options and places to go to meet girls, the USY dance felt rather restrictive. However, all the people we'd met at these dances over the years started to have house parties. And those house parties often had beer. No dance, USY or otherwise, could live up to that.

One such party that I attended was at the home of a girl named Sarah whom I had met on several occasions over the years. My buddies and I jumped into the station wagon and made the twenty-minute trip to Sarah's house full of hopes and expectations. I mean alcohol + Jewish girls. Was there a better combination to be found for a young Semite like myself?

When we arrived, the party was already in full swing. Around 50 people or so crammed into Sarah's folks' living room, dining room and kitchen. A full keg had been tapped and placed out on the back porch for all to enjoy. There was only one problem: They were out of plastic keg cups. Undaunted, I opened a few cabinets hoping to find a glass or a mug. Hell, I would have settled for a "My Pretty Pony" collector's cup, anything that would hold liquid. However, Sarah had (wisely) removed all the glassware from the cabinets to prevent breakage and/or theft.

I was stuck. How was I going to get my rap (feeble though it may have been) going without a frosted barley lubricant? After searching the kitchen, I grabbed the only available container I could find: The 64 oz. Pyrex coffee pot. Strolling casually through the crowd, Mr. Coffee and I made our way out to the back porch and the sweet, amber nectar it promised. As I poised the spigot over the wide mouth of the pot and prepared to release its contents, someone grabbed my arm with the force of an iron claw.

"What the HELL do you think you're doing?!?!?" screamed Sarah. All at once, the party noise stopped.

"I...well...you were out of cups...and I thought..." I stammered weakly.

"Put that back in the kitchen where it belongs RIGHT NOW!" she roared.

"I...sure...can I just fill it up a little?"

"NO!!!!!!"

"I was gonna wash it out."

"NOW!!!!"

Turning three shades of crimson, I skulked back to the kitchen and replaced the coffee pot. Sarah had followed me.

"Why don't you and your friends leave now," she said in a tone that implied that this was not a request, but an order.

"Look, I'm sorry..." I began.

"Please leave," she repeated, unmoved.

So, my buddies and I retreated down the steps and out onto the front lawn while the door slammed shut behind us.

Suddenly, my friend Mike became indignant.

"She can't talk to you like that!" he declared.

"Well, I did try to fill her parents' coffee pot with beer," I admitted.

"So what? This is a party," he shot back. "What does she expect?"

"Let's just go," I said.

"No, not without something to remember this by," Mike vowed.

And with that, he bounded up the front steps and pried off the nameplate that was tacked just above the doorbell. Raising it in triumph like the sword of Excalibur, he boomed, "That'll show her!"

Cheering, we ran to the car and sped home with our treasure. Mike insisted that I keep it as a memento of the culmination of our careers, for that was the last USY event we would ever attend.

I kept the nameplate on my desk for years, studying it often and laughing at the futility of our adolescent gesture. Many years later, in a twist of O. Henry-esque irony, Sarah and my wife became friends independent of me. The first time we got together as couples, Sarah and I did the math and recalled that ridiculous night of so long ago. She had often wondered what had happened to the nameplate and we shared a good chuckle when I admitted my part in its theft.

Today, Sarah's family and mine are very close. I've heard her yell at her children (and her husband) in times of stress, but she's never matched the intensity or fury with which she yelled at me that night.

In one final bit of sitcom coincidence, I've also come to know and admire Sarah's parents. And if, by some chance, they happen to read this, I can only say: I owe you a doorbell nameplate.

*

The Jewfro Monologues

Growing up, my greatest desire in life was to have long hair. I didn't care about fame or fortune. I didn't dream about power or prominence. I just wanted long, flowing locks. Back then, long hair stood for something important. It stood for rock and roll.

When grown-ups spotted a man with long hair they would inevitably think of him as a derelict or remark that he looked like a girl. Not me. I saw a rebel. I saw a free thinker. I saw the man that I wanted to become.

By the turn of the decade (the decade being the 1980s) rock and roll was under assault. Punk, disco and new wave conspired to make rock and roll seem dated and irrelevant. But for us, the last generation raised on The Beatles and the Stones, on Zeppelin and the Who, we still held on to the dream. We wanted to live the idealized lifestyle of sex, drugs and rock and roll. Sure, sex wasn't happening and allergy shots were the drugs of choice, but we could still rock.

And nothing said rock and roll more than long hair.

Once I was old enough to throw off the shackles of my mother's stylistic tendencies – she who seemed to favor the Prince Valiant haircut and polyester jumpsuits for her boys – I knew that I would immediately commence OPERATION: LONG HAIR. I figured that I'd hit shoulder-length by 15 and Crystal Gayle by graduation.

And then a funny, horrible thing happened. My hair,

finally given the chance to grow DOWN decided to grow OUT. It was clear that I had the curse of our people – the dreaded Jewfro.

I should have known better. One of our favorite family stories involved a young Woodstock-era uncle, a bottle of hair relaxer and some panty hose. What a fool I was to think that I could break the curse and achieve the long hair. Nope, the closest that I would come to being rock and roll was Art Garfunkel.

In other words, not very rock and roll at all.

As my Jewfro grew, I began to resent it more and more. Every mousse, gel and random cream that I found in my father's vanity failed to tame the beast. All of my academic, athletic and romantic failures could be traced back to that accursed Jewfro. That goddamn chia pet on top of my skull was the bane of my existence.

Luckily, over time I began to accept my lot in life. Sure, I'd have moments of delusion where I'd try to grow my hair out and convince myself that it looked good, or I'd get angry and cut it too short. But time has a way of softening the hurts of life and I began to embrace the ironic use of facial hair to compensate for my inability to do anything even remotely cool with my hair.

Of course, time also has a way of teaching you painful lessons, and as my forehead continues to grow and my hairline continues to shrink, I've begun to miss that old Jewfro. We sure had some good times together. And while long hair is clearly better than a Jewfro, a sweet Jewfro is assuredly better than being bald.

So, some advice to our young male readers: don't hate your Jewfro. Celebrate it. Love it. Revel in it. Because, as the saying goes, you don't know what you've got 'til it's gone.

And besides, Bob Dylan has always sported an amazing Jewfro, and you can't get any more rock and roll than that.

*

I Was A Hebrew High School Dropout

When my Bar-Mitzvah had come and gone and the last thank-you note had been written, I stood in my parents' kitchen and gave a little cheer.

"What was that for?" asked my mother.

"I'm done," I replied. "No more Hebrew school. No more waking up early on Sundays. No more after school Torah study. No more missing basketball and baseball practice."

"Oh, you're not done, mister," my father countered. "We signed you up for Hebrew High School."

"W-what?!?" I stammered.

"That's right. You're going to Hebrew High School. It's only once a week on Sunday for three hours. Mike and Robbie are going too," my mother said.

"But, that's not fair!" I yelled, regaining my voice as well as a healthy dose of righteous indignation. "I did everything I was supposed to do. I don't want to go to Hebrew School anymore."

"It's not Hebrew School. It's Hebrew High School," corrected my mother.

"But…"

"Here's the deal," my father said, cutting me off. "You'll go for a semester and if you don't like it you can stop at the end of December. We think it'll make you more well-rounded."

They always played the "well-rounded" card whenever they made me do something I didn't want to do. It usually led to me rebelling violently against whatever was being foisted upon me. The two years of failed piano lessons and the dust-covered Baldwin Upright in the living room was tangible evidence of that. But, I also knew there was no sense in arguing. So, I trudged off to Temple Mishkan Tefila one bright Sunday morning in September with the equally ill-tempered Mike and Robbie by my side.

I will say this, the first thing I noticed were the girls. There were all these new (and pretty) faces from Jewish communities all over the Boston area. However, just like in real high school, these Hebrew hotties were only interested in the upperclassmen. So, after getting no play from the ladies (as usual) I headed off to class.

In fairness, the courses might have been appealing if I weren't so determined not to like them. The subjects included Jewish philosophy, Talmudic interpretation and Modern Judaism. The teachers ranged from cranky to engaging and the dialogue was somewhat interesting.

But, every time I felt like applying myself I remembered that I was there against my will. So, I went to class, did the bare minimum of work and served that first semester like a prison sentence.

When the December holidays rolled around, I marched into my father's office, set my textbooks on his desk and made the following declaration:

"The first semester is over. I tried Hebrew High School. I do not like it. I am done."

"No you're not," he replied evenly. "We paid for the whole year and you're going for the whole year."

"But, that's not fair!" I exploded. "We had a deal!"

"CJ," my father proclaimed, "if the Jews can wander through the desert for 40 years, you can go to Hebrew High School for one more semester."

And with that, the matter was closed. But, this time when I went back to Mishkan Tefila after the holidays I was determined to get into trouble. I vowed to be the worst student in Hebrew High School history. If they were going to make me go, I was going to make them sorry.

Thus, my one-man campaign to become a Jewish juvenile delinquent, a "Jew-linquent" if you will, began. On the first day back after break, I got myself thrown out of a Torah study class for repeatedly talking out of turn. In regular school, I had never even gotten detention much less been tossed out of class. But, as I sat by myself in the hallway waiting for the next class I had an epiphany (which is an odd thing for a Jewish kid to have). I realized that there were no consequences for misbehaving in Hebrew High School. The worst thing they could do was expel me, which was precisely what I wanted. This was the best kind of rebellion, the kind where you could act up without fear of punishment.

Armed with this knowledge, I became the bad boy of Mishkan Tefila. I routinely skipped at least one class every Sunday, using the hour to walk over to a nearby bagel store for a morning snack. In the classes I didn't skip I actively tried to get myself thrown out for cracking jokes or chewing gum or pretending to be asleep. And homework? Forget about it. Never touched the stuff.

Toward the end of the semester, the principal asked to speak with me in her office. There was some doubt, she told me, whether I would be allowed to return in the fall. Solemnly, I replied that I was prepared to accept whatever decision the school saw fit to make. Meanwhile, in my head I knew there was no way I was coming back even if the school offered me a teaching position.

My parents were mildly disappointed, but not surprised when I told them that the great Hebrew High School experiment was officially over no matter how many years the Jews wandered in the desert. Then, later that year, I ran into one of the pretty girls from Mishkan Tefila at a dance.

"Weren't you the guy who used to get kicked out of class in Hebrew High School?" she asked.

"Why, yes I was," I replied suavely.

"You were a real jerk," she said, walking away.

Perhaps, I thought to myself. But, at least I was a jerk who finally got to sleep late on Sundays.

*

The Chairwoman

My mother has always been afraid of heights. This includes, but is not limited to, airplanes, tall buildings, glass elevators and spiral staircases. (I always thought she would have been great as the Kim Novak character in *Vertigo*. Both she and James Stewart would have been totally freaking out while they climbed the bell tower, which would have made a tremendous ending as they fought each other to get back down the stairs.)

Now, acrophobia is a very real fear and I'm not about to make fun of anybody who suffers from it. But, I have to say that my mother's case certainly qualifies as amusing. You see, in addition to those other examples of altitude that I listed above, my mother is also afraid of going up on the chair during the Hora.

My family first learned of this when I got engaged. Sitting around with my bride-to-be, my brother Dan and my parents one evening in the early stages of the wedding planning, my mother stood up and declared that she was not, under any circumstances, going up in the chair after Lisa and I took our turn. The discussion stopped cold and we all looked at her quizzically. It took a full beat before we even registered what she was saying.

"You mean you're not going up in the chair with Dad?" I asked.

"He can go for both of us. I'm not interested," she replied.

Neither Dan nor I had done the chair thing for our Bar-Mitzvahs, so this was the first time we'd been faced with this controversy. He and I looked at each other briefly and then burst into gales of hysterical laughter.

"This is awesome! This is the best!" howled Dan as tears streamed from his eyes.

"Mom, you've gotta be kidding," I interjected, regaining my composure.

"I'm not kidding," answered my mom. "I am 100% serious."

"All right, you two idiots. Knock it off," growled my father as Dan and I were overtaken by a fresh set of the giggles. "She doesn't have to go up in the chair if she doesn't want to."

So, of course, from that point forward it became the running joke leading up to the wedding. My brother and I were merciless, needling my mom at every opportunity. We told her that it was Jewish law that she had to go up in the chair. We told her that it was an insult to the bride's family if she didn't go up in the chair. We told her that my dad couldn't go up solo or he'd have to fast for 40 days. (At this point, we were just making shit up to see how far we could push it.)

To her credit, my mother remained resolute. Despite our goading, she quietly maintained her stance that it didn't matter whether she went up in the chair or not. So, she wasn't going up in the chair, thank you very much. End of story. Good night. Drive home safely.

Try as we might, we couldn't get a rise out of her. Until one night, we went too far. We had just finished getting fitted for our tuxedos and decided to grab some dinner at a nearby Chinese buffet. My dad was out of town and Lisa was working, so it was just my mom, my brother and me. As we sat down to our first plate of food, Dan started in with our familiar chorus.

"You know, Mom," he said around a mouthful of boneless spareribs, "you really should go up in the chair."

"It's funny you should mention that, Dan," replied my mother crisply. "Because I talked to the rabbi and he said that the mother of the groom only goes up in the chair after her last son is married."

I nearly spit hot tea across the table.

"What?!?" I half-yelled. "He did not say that!"

"Yes, he did. He said 'only after the last son is married.'"

"Mom, you're making that up," said Dan, wading in.

"No, it's the truth."

Dan and I couldn't control ourselves any longer. We just started laughing uproariously and repeating bits of her story to each other. "Talked to the rabbi, ha-ha-ha, only when the last son is married, ha-ha-ha, mother of the groom, ha-ha-ha…"

"I AM NOT GOING UP IN THE FUCKING CHAIR!!!!!!!"

All conversation in the half-full restaurant stopped. A fork clattered to the floor. Birds flew en masse from the rooftop. A small child began to cry. And a waiter dropped a full pitcher of ice water into a customer's lap as my mother's final decree on the matter reverberated off the dragon tapestry-covered walls.

I'm not sure if anyone said a word for the rest of the meal. From that day forward, neither Dan nor I mentioned the chair or the Hora again. At the actual wedding, my mother took no chances. The video shows Lisa and me being hoisted toward the ceiling followed by my father (at a significantly lower height) and my in-laws. During the Hora, the camera briefly turns to scan the crowd and in that time you can clearly see a helmet of blond hair flash quickly through the scene and then exit through the function hall door. If Zapruder had shot wedding videos, this would have been his finest moment.

My mother did not go up in the chair.

Epilogue

My brother got married over thirteen years after I walked down the aisle. As the wedding approached, our old refrain found its voice.

"You know, Mom," I started, "Dan is the last son to get married and we all know what that means."

"I don't think so," hedged my mom.

"You promised," Dan pressed.

"We'll see," she said.

The last scene of my brother's wedding video shows my mom and dad being held aloft by half the wedding party as the other half circles wildly around them clapping and cheering.

As the chairs are returned to terra firma, my mother stands up and clutches my father both of them laughing with pure joy. At that second, the photographer snapped his shutter and captured the moment forever.

It's one of my favorite pictures of all time.

*

Talkin' Jersey

New Jersey is home to a surprising number of infamous phenomena. You've got organized crime, both real and imagined (I'm looking at you Tony Soprano). You've got corruption in government (there are more state officials in prison than in office). And, just for good measure, you've got Orthodox rabbis selling human organs and fake Gucci bags on the black market (at retail prices, no less).

Of course, The Garden State was also the home of my beautiful wife when I first met her over twenty years ago. When she took me home to meet her family early on in our relationship, I was introduced to yet another New Jersey marvel. I call it the Jersey Jive. It's a speech pattern that seems to be unique to the Meadowlands set. Sure, the New Jersey accent is nearly identical to the Noo Yawk drawl. But, it's the way they say things (or don't say things, in many cases) that is the telling difference.

When we were sitting at breakfast on that first morning in my future in-laws' kitchen, a delectable spread of Manhattan bagels and lox in front of us, I asked Lisa's sister if she wanted the cream cheese.

"No," she said. "I got."

I got?

Got what? Got milk? Well, no. Clearly I understood her to mean that she already had cream cheese. But, why "I got?" I'd been around enough people from the tri-state area to know that they truncate everything. Like they don't have enough time to even finish their thoughts. But, if that were the case, why didn't she just say, "I have." As in, "I already have some."

I thought that maybe, as an obnoxious English major, I was being overly critical. But, then we were out in Boston with some of my friends and someone asked Lisa if she wanted some nachos.

"I got," she answered.

All conversation stopped. As a single unit, all my buddies turned on her.

"Whaddaya mean 'you got,' they demanded? You got what?

"Do I really say that?" Lisa asked, blushing.

"Your whole family says it," I told her gently.

When she told her parents about our night out, her mom refused to believe it.

"We do not say 'I got,' she maintained.

About five minutes later I asked her if she wanted a diet soda.

"No, I got," she responded automatically and then slapped her hand over her mouth.

The other great Jersey conceit is asking a question in

the negative when you are clearly looking for a positive response.

"You're going to the mall, no?"

"You like Chinese food, no?"

"You've seen *Dr. No*, no?"

My wife still does this even after living in the Boston area for over fifteen years. But, she gets mad if I point it out or do it myself in mock imitation of her. And it really pisses her off when I get the kids to do it. The other day, our three-year-old was sitting at the kitchen table when he looked up innocently and said, "Mommy, you're making me oatmeal, no?"

Look, I know that Boston is famous for its linguistic idiosyncrasies. But, to my ear, the Jersey Jive stands out like a Red Sox fan in Yankee Stadium.

Maybe I just need more exposure to New Jersey culture to fully appreciate the language, no?

On second thought, I got.

*

The Complaints Department

"Young may-an! Youuuuuu ahr a guest he-ya!" a shrill voice screeched at me from across the exercise room.

"I beg your pardon, ma'am?" I replied in my most innocent tone.

"You ahr a guest he-ya and it is yahr responsibility to wipe down the equipment after you use it," pressed the voice, which belonged to a 60-something woman with brassy red hair, ill-fitting spandex pants and a Noo Yawk attitude.

The other half-dozen or so seniors in the room looked up from their treadmills and yoga balls to see who the offending party was. Feeling cornered, I quickly acquiesced.

"I was just about to, ma'am," I said, grabbing a paper towel and earnestly dabbing at the sit-up bench that had been dusty from disuse until I had lain on it just a few moments before.

Fixing me with a final glare, Red went back to climbing imaginary hills on her Exer-Cycle. I shouldn't have been surprised at the treatment I received. After all, this wasn't my first trip to the clubhouse that my in-laws shared with several hundred other 55+ people in their Adult Living community.

With both children out of the house and starting

families of their own, my wife's parents eschewed the Florida game plan when they retired. Instead, they bought a plot of land in a planned development, chose one of the five models that were offered to them and built a house that was ultimately bigger than the home they had lived in for over 30 years. Except now, it was just the two of them.

Developments like theirs have been popping up all over the Northeast for the past ten or fifteen years. I have to admit, it's a brilliant idea. Find cheap land on the fringe of a commuter zone, build a 9-hole, Par 3 golf course, surround it with large cookie-cutter houses that will easily accommodate visiting children and grandchildren, drop in a clubhouse with an indoor and outdoor pool, tennis courts, card room, aerobics studio/gym and an arts & crafts suite and voila, you've got an instant Adult Living community.

For retired and semi-retired Northeasterners who don't want to snowbird or just want to stay close to family and friends, it's an attractive option. You can find a poker, bridge, canasta or mah-jongg game every night. There are social clubs, eating clubs, knitting clubs and even drama clubs. It's like summer camp for the senior set. And if you want to go into the city for business or pleasure once or twice a week, it isn't such a hardship to get on the train for an hour. The only thing missing is the year-round nice weather. But, when you have all this, who cares? It's ideal.

Except for one thing.

What those pioneering developers failed to take into account was that by building these communities they were taking a large number of people whose favorite pastime is complaining and putting them all in one place.

I don't know how much money the builders made off their original investment. But, even if it was in the tens of millions, it can't possibly be enough to justify the sheer number of complaints they field on a daily basis. Even with my limited involvement during the building process, I heard that the floors were wrong, the cabinets were too small (then they were too big), the fixtures were off and the lights were too bright. (This last problem was fixed with the addition of something I like to call a "dimmer.") And this was only one of the 200 or so houses in the original development. Worse still for these poor bastards, the new residents would call each other daily to describe what was currently wrong in their respective homes. This would prompt people to check their houses to see if they, too, had the same problem as their neighbors so that they could add it to their list.

Now some of you might be thinking that my in-laws and their friends had every right to be picky about their new homes since they were paying a lot of money to the developers. And you'd be right if, in fact, it ended there. However, the complaining during the building process was merely an appetizer, an amuse-bouche if you will, for what was to come.

Their homes completed to their satisfaction (or as near to that as one could hope to come), the residents turned their attention to the facilities. The clubhouse was the first amenity to come under attack. Its small weight room had been outfitted with several treadmills, stair climbers and recumbent bikes. However, the builders had bought the kind for personal use rather than industrial, heavy-duty use like the ones you'd find in a Gold's Gym. I guess they figured the older ladies and gentlemen of the community wouldn't tax the apparatus any more than a single soccer mom would in her basement. Well, they figured wrong.

When the first treadmill broke down, the hue and cry was so great that a special committee was formed to get the machines replaced. The builders complied and then the slippery slope to hell began to tip downward. The committee, seeing its power, began to make demands on a regular basis.

Everyone was unhappy with the water fountains in the gym, so they brought in a water cooler. Then, people complained that the 5-gallon bottles were too heavy to lift onto the cooler, so it became the janitor's responsibility to replace the bottles when they were empty. But, the janitor often waited days to replace bottles because he was busy doing other things. Like cleaning. So, the committee made the developers bring in a water purifying machine that didn't require a 5-gallon bottle. However, the little paper cups that came with the machine ran out frequently and weren't being refilled often enough. So, everybody just went back to using the water fountains.

From the gym, the committee (now growing

exponentially in members) marched on the indoor pool where they imposed a strict schedule on the lap swimmers and water aerobicists who were warring over space in the super-heated water. Both factions, however, were overruled by the politically powerful men's water volleyball team, which commanded the entire pool three times a week during prime swimming hours. There was universal accord, though, on the Grandchild Rule stating that no un-toilet trained child shall be allowed in the pool ever. Ironic considering what many of those seniors were surely doing in the pool themselves.

Complaining reaches a fever pitch in the summertime when the golf course, tennis courts and outdoor pool are all open. The gang just about blows a gasket when someone isn't wearing a collared shirt on the driving range. In fact, one of the club pros lost his job when it was discovered that he allowed someone to hit a bucket of balls in a t-shirt. The tennis crowd is a little more tolerant unless you book a court before noon without the presence of a resident. In that case, bring your boxing gloves because you're gonna have to fight your way out of there. And if kids are splashing in the pool or making too much noise, you can be sure that a lifeguard will be dispatched to quite the rabble-rousers. (Have you ever known a child who didn't splash or make noise in a pool? What the hell else are you supposed to do in a pool when you're six?)

The best complaint moment of all time came when they opened the new and improved gym. My father-in-law, who never uses the gym, went down to check out the new facility. After walking around for a few minutes, he determined that the entrance was too drafty and would chill the people on the Stair Climbers (the same Stair Climbers upon which he had never set foot). After he and a few others complained, they put up a half-wall between the entrance and the Stair Climbers. He hasn't been back since.

On a recent visit to my in-laws, I ran into my old nemesis, Red, in the gym one morning.

"How are you, ma'am?" I inquired, trying to make nice.

"Oh, I can't complain," she replied.

"Yeah, right," I said.

But not loud enough for her to hear.

*

The Chosen Brands

When I was a kid, my mother nearly started a civil war when she made my father an egg salad sandwich using Miracle Whip.

"What the hell is crap?!?" my father growled, spitting chunks of egg salad back onto his plate.

"Egg salad," my mother replied, clearly taken aback. "Just like you asked for."

"What did you use for mayonnaise?" demanded my father.

"Miracle Whip. It was on sa-"

"Never bring that garbage into this house again! It's goyisha mayonnaise."

Up until that point in my childhood, I didn't know that food could have a religion. But, it soon became clear to me that certain brands were favored by Jewish people while other brands were, to euphemize the words of my father, for those of other faiths.

In this essay, I want to discuss three such food arguments that pit a "Jewish" brand versus a "non-Jewish" brand. I know I'm only scratching the surface here, but these three examples seem to come up time and time again whenever the subject is raised.

1. <u>Hellmann's vs. Miracle Whip</u>

To hear my father tell it, Miracle Whip doesn't even qualify as mayonnaise. And, in his defense, it actually says "Salad Dressing" on the side of the jar. I'm not a big mayo guy, but I will say that Hellmann's has a little tanginess to it while Miracle Whip is simply white paste. Not to mention the fact that Kraft Foods, the maker of Miracle Whip, is one of the most goyisha companies in the US. Everything they make seems to be geared to the blandest of palates.

Now, there are a lot of people who will say that the mayo argument transcends the Jewish vs. non-Jewish preference. These people will claim that this is a New York/New England thing. New Englanders (excluding those south of Hartford, CT) prefer Miracle Whip while metropolitan New York, New Jersey and southern Connecticut favor Hellmann's. My mother, who is a dyed-in-the-wool Yankee from Newton, MA and says things like "haaf" and "bahthroom" when she means half and bathroom, grew up on Kraft's version of mayo. My father, on the other hand, hails from New Haven, CT and says "praid" and "You-ston" when he means parade and San Antonio. He believes that Hellmann's is the only brand that deserves to call itself mayonnaise.

Whichever side you land on, there's one thing upon which we can all agree: The fact that my parents are insane.

2. Gulden's vs. French's

Now, here's a debate I am truly passionate about. For the simple reason that I hate French's mustard with the heat of a thousand suns. It is the worst of all that mustard has to offer-thin, acerbic and drippy. It even has the self-awareness to call itself "Yellow" mustard as if it were cowardly, afraid to provide a sandwich with any hint of flavor or zest. And, if you are unfortunate enough to get any of it on your clothing, the stain will never, ever come completely out.

Gulden's, by contrast, is everything mustard is supposed to be. Thick, dark, bursting with all the richness of the mustard seeds from which it came. You can put it on deli, burgers, hot dogs, pretzels, even chicken and fish. (My wife bastes sole and cod in a mixture of Hellmann's and Gulden's before cooking it. You can imagine how happy this makes me.) Most Jewish delis have Gulden's on every table as a matter of course. You won't find French's in any deli worth its salt because no deli that cared about its products would allow you to defile them with "Yellow" mustard. For that reason, you won't find French's in many Jewish homes either.

To put an end to this one-sided debate once and for all, consider this: A few years ago, French's added a brown mustard to its product line that tasted like a poor man's Gulden's. Of course, Gulden's has yet to put out a yellow mustard or anything other than their original brown mustard, for that matter. And if you're waiting for them to do so, don't hold your breath.

3) <u>Temp Tee vs. Philadelphia</u>

If you're Jewish, what you put on your bagel is of the utmost importance. If you use butter, you're probably an Episcopalian. If you use jelly, you're probably a child. If you use cream cheese, you might be Jewish. But, it's your brand of choice that will likely be the deciding factor.

Temp Tee, Breakstone's whipped cream cheese product, has been in nearly every Jewish home I've ever entered. It's creamy, yet not too heavy, and it holds lox, tomatoes and onions really well. Going to a brunch and finding Temp Tee on the table is very reassuring. It makes me think that the omelet station may not run out of eggs half an hour into the meal.

Philadelphia cream cheese is a good enough product, but I would not be surprised to learn that it was 100% synthetic. It's got that sort of plastic sheen that I do not feel belongs on my bagel. Not to mention that I've seen it break knives on occasion. Philly appears best suited to cheesecake or other foods which require solid blocks of cream cheese that don't need to be, well, spread.

Using our Gulden's corollary, Philadelphia now has a product that is a lot like Temp Tee. But, Temp Tee doesn't have anything that resembles Philly. And while most Jewish people will use Philly in a pinch, they wouldn't give it a second glance if Temp Tee were an option. Ultimately, we're talking about what goes on the bread of our people. Trust me. Go with the stuff in the pink container.

These are just three examples of what some would consider Jewish brands as opposed to non-Jewish brands. It's just a matter of opinion, though. There's no such thing as a brand that's 100% Jewish. Except for Manischewitz. Those guys are hardcore.

*

I'll See Your Banh Mi and Raise You a Chacarero (Introducing the Chazer Mekheye)

While the rest of you are wasting time making personal improvement resolutions, I'm kicking off the year by coming up with new and exciting schemes for securing global fame and fortune.

I'm thinking that inventing this year's hot new sandwich might be a good angle.

It seems like each and every year a new sandwich takes America by storm and what could possibly be easier than: 1) inventing a delicious sandwich that's never been thought of before, 2) opening a restaurant that sells the aforementioned sandwich, 3) garnering many positive reviews in the media and creating an insatiable demand, 4) franchising the whole operation and 5) retiring on a houseboat with all of my delectable sandwich money?

Last year's big sandwich was the Vietnamese concoction known as the Banh Mi. A Banh Mi is a baguette filled with pickled carrots and radishes, cilantro, cucumbers, mayo, and literally anything else that can be jammed into the bread: meat, eggs, old newspapers, whatever. Now, that may sound disgusting, but the Banh Mi was the perfect sandwich for the Great Recession: it's super-cheap and it has a cool name (banh mi means 'bread' in Vietnamese. Methinks that "bread sandwich" is somewhat less catchy than banh mi.)

So there are the first two pieces of the puzzle: our

new sandwich for 2011 needs to be cheap and it needs a cool name.

In Boston we have the truly awesome chacarero sandwich, which is allegedly a traditional Chilean sandwich. (I say allegedly because no one has ever been to Chile to confirm its provenance, or for that matter, to confirm that Chile really exists.) The chacarero features homemade bread (kind of a cross between a roll and a pita), green beans, avocado, tomatoes, muenster cheese, hot sauce and either beef or chicken (or both). The chacarero is very popular and commands impossibly long lines at lunchtime.

Studying the Chacarero gives us two more secrets for creating the perfect sandwich: the crucial role of good bread and the need for a mysterious origin/back story.

Many of you may be familiar with the wrap sandwich. While tasty, the wrap sandwich represents cultural imperialism of the worst kind. You see, the wrap is nothing more than a bastardized burrito. A good burrito is a wonderful thing – the perfect lunch that's just big enough to ruin dinner and set you up for a night of early dessert gorging. But the reason that the wrap will never be cool is because people seek authenticity, and there's nothing authentic about a burrito made out of tuna fish. Our perfect sandwich will most assuredly be authentic.

Finally, we must also remember to include bacon. "Vegetarian's kryptonite" as I like to call it – bacon is the perfect food. The problem with bacon, of course, is that everyone knows that it's bad for you. As a result, people feel guilty when adding it to their sandwiches. Our challenge is to include bacon on our sandwich without making people feel guilty about ordering it.

So there you have it. The big idea sandwich for 2011 needs to:

1) Be cheap ($5 maximum)

2) Have a cool name (i.e. not English)

3) Feature good bread (no seeds or oats or grains or weird shit)

4) Possess a mysterious back story (think J. Peterman)

5) Be authentic

6) Include bacon (but not that fake Canadian stuff)

Introducing...The Chazer Mekheye

In ancient times, a small but forgotten tribe of Jews, known only as the Hogakanazi, fought the rabbinical authority and refused to consider the world's most delicious animal, the pig, as treif (or non-kosher). These brave Jews spent thousands of years in hiding, honing and refining the perfect sandwich – known only as the Chazer Mekheye – as a symbol of their devotion and solidarity.

The dying wish of the last of the Hogakanazis was to finally share this incredible sandwich with the rest of the world. The secret of the Chazer Mekheye was entrusted to just one man – me – and now I will share the fruit of the Hogakanazis with you. I invite you to experience this nearly-forgotten culinary delicacy.

Each Chazer Mekheye is lovingly hand-crafted on our unique artisan Hogakanzi bacon-infused bagel, with a dab of horseradish mayonnaise, crisp leaf lettuce, vine-ripened tomato, Vidalia onion and your choice of beef, chicken or combo. All for just $5.

The Chazer Mekheye. It's so good you might just plotz.

*

Shut Up and Eat

Siblings will fight over anything. That's just a fact of life. The desire to come out ahead of one's kin in any argument, physical competition or intellectual challenge is so great that entire wars have been fought because some kid wanted two square feet more land than his brother. (Note: I don't know if this is actually true, but it works for my analogy. Hey, if you want facts, watch The History Channel.)

My own brother and I took sibling rivalry to an entirely new and completely insane level. Sure, Dan and I would battle it out for supremacy on the basketball court or match wits across a game board, but where the claws really came out was at the kitchen table. We would actually compete over food. Not over who could eat the most, but over who could eat last.

You see, Dan had this thing about always wanting to be the last one to finish his food. He had to have the last bite of the meal or he would go ballistic. I didn't care much when I finished as long as I was full. But every once in a while, just to torque Dan, I'd linger over the last few morsels on my plate.

"What are you doing?" he'd ask suspiciously, putting down his fork.

"Nothing," I'd reply sheepishly. "Just enjoying my dinner."

"Finish it!" he'd growl between clenched teeth.

"Of course," I'd say.

Then, I'd take a small forkful of mixed vegetables, put them in my mouth and chew 100-200 times before swallowing. By this time, Dan would be purple with rage.

"Stop screwing around and finish it!"

"But, Dan, you know how important it is to chew your food carefully. Helps with digestion."

Smiling, I'd then pick up my napkin with a flourish and dab my chin. Dan would be across the table with fists flying before I could even pretend to be surprised.

However, when Yom Kippur rolled around our internecine food feud would amp up considerably. As maniacal as Dan was about eating last for 364 days a year, he was even more obsessive about not eating first on the 365th.

Before we were Bar-Mitzvahed, our parents made it optional for us to fast on (cue big, echo-y voice) THE DAY OF ATONEMENT! Dan and I would try to make it through the day, but we'd inevitably succumb around 3 or 4 o'clock after seeing half a dozen Pizza Hut commercials. Even then, Dan couldn't let it go. We'd agree that we were going to break the fast early and then go into the kitchen and open a package of Oreos.

"Take a bite," Dan would say, offering me a cookie.

Sensing his desperation, I would demure.

"You first."

"No, you!"

"I think you should go first. After all, it was your idea."

Dan's nostrils would flare, his hunger fueling his anger.

"EAT IT!"

"You know what? I'm not hungry anymore."

Turning my back (a mistake), I'd walk nonchalantly out of the kitchen. With a primal scream, Dan would grab an Oreo and chase me around the house trying to cram it into my mouth the entire time. This would continue until my parents sent both of us to our rooms enveloped in the shame of having committed the ultimate sin. We'd misbehaved on THE DAY OF ATONEMENT!

Looking back, I see the humor in two pre-teen boys trying to best each other in something as ridiculous as fasting. It's cute, even a little charming. What wasn't charming was the way this contest escalated during our post Bar-Mitzvah years.

Now obligated to fast for the full day, Dan and I

needed something to vie for. The answer was obvious. In fact, we both arrived at the same conclusion simultaneously. It happened as the last rays of light disappeared beneath the horizon one Yom Kippur evening.

"Boys!" called my mother from the kitchen. "Come on down and have something to eat! The fast is over!"

Dan and I rumbled into the kitchen and instantly began to drool over the spread of bagels, cream cheese, lox and noodle kugel. We sat down at the table, filled our plates and each poured a tall, cold glass of orange juice.

Then, just as we were about to dig in, we looked up at each other.

"Go ahead," said Dan.

"Nah, you go ahead," I replied.

We stared at each other resolutely, neither willing to take that first sweet sip of juice or glorious mouthful of bagel.

"Hey, I just realized something," I began, breaking the silence. "I think you're supposed to wait until there are three stars in the sky before you break the fast. I'll go check to see if they're up there."

"I'll go with you," said Dan, getting up from the table.

"You two are idiots," declared my dad as he shoveled spoonfuls of egg salad into his mouth.

The two of us went out the front door and onto the driveway, craning our necks toward the inky black sky. Unfortunately for us a front had moved in causing complete cloud cover. There wasn't a single star visible, let alone three.

Walking back into the house, we took our seats at the table and resumed our stalemate. Meanwhile, my dad was on his second bagel and his third helping of kugel.

"See any stars, Copernicus?" chortled my dad around a mouthful of lox.

Ignoring him, we continued our stare-down.

"I think I'm going to wait another half hour just to be safe," I volleyed.

"Me too," agreed Dan. "Just to be safe."

"All right, that's enough!" spat my dad. "Both of you pick up your orange juice. Now, on the count of three, drink. Whoever doesn't is grounded for a week. One…two…three."

Dan and I looked at each other one last time, raised our glasses to our lips and sipped.

"Good," pronounced my dad. "Now eat."

Without further hesitation, Dan and I dove into the now depleted spread.

I wish I could say this was the last time we had such a standoff, but anyone who knows us has already guessed that it wasn't. This scenario played out in some form or another every year until I went to college. And even then, Dan would call me in my dorm room at sundown on THE DAY OF ATONEMENT and ask if I had eaten yet.

I'd lie and say I had and he'd do the same and we'd both hang up hungry, but satisfied.

*

Opening a Can of Crazy for Mother's Day

Let's get something straight. I love my mom. Lord knows, without her this book wouldn't exist. In fact, the things that she said and did when I was growing up almost certainly led to me becoming a writer. It was the most lucrative form of therapy that I could come up with to offset the insanity of my childhood. But, just when I thought I'd seen every form of crazy my mom had to offer, she took her game to another level.

Those of you in the Boston area will be familiar with the water crisis we had in May of 2010. For those outside the 617, here's the story: It seems that a rather large pipe carrying water from the crystal clear reservoirs of central Massachusetts to us heathens here inside Route 128, for lack of a better explanation, broke. Actually, it pretty much disintegrated. Which resulted in millions of gallons of untreated water coursing through the pipes of Beantown and thirty-odd surrounding communities. So, the local officials issued a proclamation that everyone in the affected areas needed to boil their water for at least a minute before drinking it.

Now, the broken pipe in question was located in the town of Weston, MA, which meant that all the water west of the break was still okay to drink. Indeed, it was probably the best water in the state for those three days. I mention this because we met my parents for lunch that Sunday in Framingham, a full two towns west of the breach. And that's where my mom became a legend.

This book has several entries about what our families have taken from restaurants over the years—sugar and jelly packets, napkins, straws, extra Peking ravioli, etc.—but I'd never given much thought to what a member of my family might bring *into* a restaurant. Until that Sunday.

As the waitress came over to our table, I looked at my mom expectantly. Watching her order is always a magical experience and she didn't disappoint that day. We were at TGI Friday's and she wanted their Cobb Salad, but with a few minor modifications. She asked the waitress to leave off the tomatoes (too acidic), the hard-boiled egg (couldn't verify its freshness), the bacon (too salty), the avocado (too exotic), the olives (ditto) and the bleu cheese (due to lactose intolerance which didn't manifest itself until she was in her mid-50s). All that was left was a few leaves of Romaine lettuce and some diced grilled chicken.

When I asked her why she ordered the Cobb salad if she didn't want 90% of what went into it, she replied with a straight face, "Oh, because Friday's makes the best Cobb salad."

"Really?" I drawled in my most obsequious tone. "What is it about Friday's Cobb salad that makes it so superior? Is it the lettuce or the chicken? And can you really, in good conscience, still call it a Cobb salad at this point?" (That last part earned me a dirty look from my mother and a stifled guffaw from my father.)

Unfazed by our one act family play, the waitress plunged on. "Do you want the dressing mixed in or on the side?"

"That won't be necessary," my mother responded. "I brought my own."

And with that she pulled from her purse a Ziploc bag with a full bottle of Ken's Italian dressing inside. Not the little bottle, but the full-on, 24 oz. supermarket bottle.

The tortilla chip I was eating fell out of my mouth and dribbled onto my plate. Did my mom carry a full bottle of Ken's Italian in her purse everyday on the off chance that she would run into an undressed salad? I looked at my dad, but he just shrugged like nothing surprised him anymore.

Our waitress blinked rapidly a couple of times, but to her credit was able to soldier on.

"Very well, ma'am," she said. "Would you like something to drink with that?"

"Oh, no," said my mother whipping a can of Diet Coke out of some other region of her purse, "I'm not drinking anything that came through the tap."

I may be exaggerating here, but it felt like all conversation stopped and the entire restaurant went stone silent.

My wife was the first adult at the table to regain the

use of her tongue.

"But, the pipe broke ten miles east of here," she said to my mother. "There's nothing wrong with the water here."

"They don't know that for sure," replied my mother as she popped open the can and took a sip. "And I'm not taking any chances."

And so, while her husband, son, daughter-in-law and grandchildren drank the questionable water of Framingham (water, I might add, that people in 38 Boston-area communities would have killed for on that Sunday), my mother swigged caffeine-laden, artificially sweetened, carbonated fizz from a silver can of safety. And did so with a look of satisfaction that suggested she had outsmarted them all.

So, as we celebrate our mothers and remember all the things they do for (and to) us, let me be the first to raise a toast to my own mother. Here's to you, Mom: For all that you bring to the table.

*

ABOUT THE AUTHORS

Way back in 1987 a young man by the name of **C.J. Kaplan** (adwriter.net) was preparing to head off to college. Before leaving, he needed to train his replacement to take over as register boy at the Waldenbooks in Needham, Massachusetts. His successor was none other than **Mitch Blum**. (mitchblum.com) C.J. taught Mitch the finer points of manning the front desk at a bookstore in a small New England town: carefully stacking the romance novels, ripping the covers off of remaindered books, and trading *Playboys* for Lime Rickeys with the guys who worked at the nearby Brigham's.

Many years later, C.J. and Mitch were reunited when they happened upon each other in the hallway at the ad agency in Boston where they both ended up working.

Like most ad folks, C.J. and Mitch have a rich history of side jobs and freelance projects. Both are gifted voice-over actors (at least according to their mothers). C.J. has won two New England Emmy Awards for his writing work on the NESN TV show *Sox Appeal*. Mitch is the co-host of the popular *Steve Gorman Sports* podcast. Neither distinction has made them rich nor famous.

Both are still recovering from the upbringing that is so lovingly described in this very book.

10731243R0